★

# CANNABIS MARKET

### 420

# CANNABIS MARKET

*by*

*Robert Robinson*

*Technical Handbook*

*First Edition*

# INTRODUCTION

Cannabis Market

*"The handbook educating enthusiasts how to properly cultivate and consume their medical marijuana or recreational cannabis products safely!"*

## Dedication

This book is dedicated to my readers, the indigenous people of the English-speaking world. From the Native Americans of the U.S., to the South Africans and even the aborigines of Oceania: This book is for you! With your help, we can finally put an end to marijuana-induced heart palpitations, breathing problems, impaired motor skills, negative thoughts and speech impairment.

Let's offer herbal remedies to those who lack a pharmaceutical answer! Your results are guaranteed to cause the rest of the Free World to follow suit.

# Foreword

As a Native American, I have known Robert since he was a young boy. I first met him while working at his stepfather's tax business. From my own personal experience, he is an honest, trustworthy, born-again Sabbatarian Christian. What he lacks in education he makes up for in firsthand experience. The professionalism and penmanship his books offer are unrivaled worldwide!

This man's diverse background also includes landscaping and accounting. His recreational marijuana use and gardening skills influenced the black market so much even cartels and local dealers began asking him for growing tips!

*-Nancy Davis*

# Preface

Cannabis Market, my sixth title, is a technical handbook for every marijuana enthusiast, both medicinal and recreational, catering both to novices and top experts. Unlike other cannabis encyclopedias, which focus on medicine and science, my handbook focuses on production, distribution, usage, reducing anxiety and overall enjoyment. Even the leaves and resin don't go to waste!

As a bonus, readers get the additional benefit of my "trip sitting" where I show them how to overcome problems with life hacks, avoid "geeking out" over them and function at their optimum level. It's done by finding balance through proper planning. One must make the right choices for certain occasions.

*Robert W. Robinson, Jr.*

-Author, TAX TREES

# TABLE OF CONTENTS

**Synopsis:**

Golden Template ............................................................ 8

**Chapter 1:**

Cannabis Homesteads ................................................... 9

**Chapter 2:**

Legendary Strains ......................................................... 17

**Chapter 3:**

Competitive Cannabis .................................................. 23

**Chapter 4:**

Natural Medications .................................................... 31

**Chapter 5:**

Factory Production ...................................................... 37

**Chapter 6:**

Inventory Management ............................................... 45

**Chapter 7:**
Organic Hydroponics .................................................. 51

**Chapter 8:**
Handcrafted Hashish ................................................. 57

**Chapter 9:**
Honey Oil Concentrates ............................................ 65

**Chapter 10:**
Paraphernalia Items .................................................. 75

**Chapter 11:**
Stationary Sessions ................................................... 81

**Chapter 12:**
Rolling Thunder ........................................................ 89

**Summary:**
The White Market .................................................... 97

**Conclusion:**
Free Enterprise ......................................................... 98

**Contributions:**
Credits & Colophon ................................................ 100

# Synopsis
## *Golden Template*

### **Domino Effect**

Consumers can only buy what's available. They lack the knowledge, experience, time, money and resources to get their hands on quality ruderalis, indica and hybrid strains to avoid anxiety. Unbeknownst to them, growers are the only individuals who steer distribution and consumption. There are two adages: Never make the customer work and keep it simple, quick and easy for them. Or, you'll talk yourself out of a sale! Therefore, presentation flows in this order: Cultivation > Distribution > Consumption.

### **Navigation**

There are four, unequally-sized quadrants. Each one is marked by a different picture on their chapters' title pages to improve navigation. The first displays a farm raising crops, second a grow lab handling product distribution, third a shop sign retailing merchandise and fourth a café catering to individual usage. Microsoft Word only lets me display a certain number of different pictures on my manuscripts and renders the rest as blank images, but it doesn't limit how many copies I can insert in each document.

### **Preview**

Chapters feature a title page, overview, group of sections and review. Title pages list the chapter's number, name, quadrant picture (for navigational reasons) and section directory. Directories display section names and page numbers. Without overviews, no one can understand any of the information sections are teaching, so don't skip them! Reviews instruct readers how to apply their newly-acquired knowledge into the real World. After the last chapter, a summary page directs readers what to do next.

# CHAPTER ONE
## *Cannabis Homesteads*

### Quadrant 1:1

*Listed below is this chapter's section directory. Topics are grouped together in subsections labeled by underlined bullets. Any further subdivision of information is organized into verses marked by bolded bullets.*

*Overview* ............................................................................ 10

*The Supply Chain* ............................................................. 11

*Cannabis Smallholdings* ................................................. 13

*Agricultural Practices* .................................................... 15

*Cultivation Techniques* .................................................. 16

*Review* ................................................................................ 18

# Overview

## Cannabis

**Weed Science 101:**

Cannabis is a genus (plural species) part of the Cannabaceae family. Its origins span across the Silk Road. This family includes hops and hackberry genera (plural genus). Further statements conflict with current classifications, but the World is wrong! Sativa, indica and ruderalis are species; the latter two aren't subspecies of sativa. Hemp is a subspecies of sativa, not a variant. Strains of these three species, like Northern Lights, are variants. Natural strains are landraces while anything manmade are crossbreeds. When strains from different species are crossbred, a hybrid is born!

**"Big Five" Cannabinoids:**

Tetrahydrocannabinol (THC) gets you stoned. I also consider tetrahydrocannabivarin (THCV) a form of THC. Cannabidiol (CBD) acts like a mild stimulant boosting energy. Cannabigerol (CBG) works with THC to create head highs. Cannabinol (CBN) reduces insomnia. Cannabichromene (CBC) increase brain cells. Everything but THC prevents anxiety, spiked heart rates or blood pressure, and difficulty breathing during sessions. They reduce seizures, mood swings, ADHD, nausea, inflammation, insomnia, cramps, impotence, arthritis pain and low metabolisms. Cannabinoids can shrink tumors too!

## Marijuana

**Autoflowers:**

Eurasian Ruderalis thrives in the cold and helped us breed autoflowers. It's tiny, fast-growing and has five-bladed leaves. Autos flower due to maturity, not light changes.

**Indica vs. Sativa:**

Indica is native to the Greater Middle East and thrives in arid regions with ease. The bushy plant fills out with wide, seven-bladed leaves. Sativa is indigenous to every continent except Antarctica and tolerates hydric (wet) often humid, environments. It's a giant in comparison to the other two and sprouts narrow, nine-bladed fan leaves.

# The Supply Chain

## Seed Banks

**Chicken and the Egg:**

During the '50s, strain hunters began collecting landrace seeds from the most remote corners of the globe. Chapter Two goes into greater detail on this subject. Eventually, we used them to produce plants dedicated to breeding the hybrids everyone has today. Thanks to their efforts, all someone must do is place an order from a reputable breeder. Seed banks should stock legendary strains and accept as many forms of payment possible. Webpages accommodate their countries' language and currency.

**Discreet Distribution:**

Station one warehouse in each country of operation resupplied by the company's headquarters depot. A customer's transactions shouldn't display any word related to cannabis on their bank statements. Discreet packages don't list a return address and seeds should be housed within their own custom-designed, protective packets. Breeders supply seed banks excess feminized and regular stockpiles. Bankers make bulk purchases letting them keep price markups affordable to remain competitive.

**Online Branches:**

Branch locations are one complex combining an office building, warehouse and parking accommodations. Staff coordinate online orders from computers. Industrial hemp plantations (50+ acres) receive parcels, smallholders (< 50 acres) packages and hobbyists plastic packets. Farmers pay 5% markups on raw materials from suppliers.

## Growers

**Cooperative Farms:**

Growers specializing in extraction form regional co-ops. In exchange for buying out members' crops and coordinating trucking runs, they rebrand everything as theirs! They communicate with trucking companies on a seasonal basis and haul goods to train stations. Farmers stuff pounds of dried, trimmed weed in one-gallon mason jars and stack them in pallets. Factories in industrial plazas pay a 10% growers' markup.

**Vertical Integration:**

Homegrown operations are vertically-integrated (all-in-one) and can do it all! They double as manufacturers too. Microdispensaries (medical/recreational combos) are miniature smoke shops (head shop/dispensary combo) resupplied by cargo vans.

# Manufacturers

**Complex Facilities:**

First, create a complex within an industrial park. Forklifts unload goods off freight trains and into garages leading to cellars. Once curing is completed, plant material is moved to press rooms where it's prepped for the next stage. Some flower becomes traditional extracts while the rest continues onward towards distillery plants. Afterwards, laboratories create isolates for solventless tinctures. Then, kitchens cook cannabutter for snacks and restaurants. Finally, warehouses serve as factory outlets.

**Cooperative Factories:**

Factories join co-ops too! They include local manufacturers, regardless of industry, and coordinate train stops. Paraphernalia makers create pipes, pipe tobacco, shisha (hookah tobacco), vaporizers, butane torches, ethanol-filled lighters, ashtrays, ash removers, lunch trays, grinders, joint rollers, cigar wraps, roach (joint butt) clips, hemp clothing and pop culture novelties. Businesses should time their shipments runs together whenever train lines arrive to save as much time and money possible.

**Factory-direct Outlets:**

American automobile manufacturers placed dozens of specialized plants together moving inventory between them constantly over short distances. This practice is called the division of labor. Unbeknownst to them, giving each region its own self-reliant factory is faster and cheaper. Office buildings coordinate online and phone orders. Manufacturers stuff pounds of hash (refined trichomes) in half-gallon jars and hash oil in quarter containers. Dro remains in its gallon jars. Wholesalers pay a 20% manufacturers' markup receiving product via railways. Outlet stores retail to locals.

# Distributors

**Regional Wholesalers:**

Everybody buying goods must show proof of owning a business, much like a Sam's Club membership. Registering a company, acquiring an EIN and obtaining permits goes a long way. DBAs don't count. Retailers pay a 40% markup on inventory, again freighted in by rail lines. Medical dispensaries are prime examples. Patients can purchase medication in person or have it mailed to them after placing online orders.

**Retail Emporiums:**

Recreational marijuana and Delta-8 hemp is shipped by rail to retailers' warehouses. Emporiums receive shipments from cargo trucks and customers are mailed packages through local carriers. Display jars: Pints (bud), cups (hash) and half-cups (oil). Dab jars: 2 oz. (rosin), 1 oz. (resin), half-oz (wax), quarter-oz (diamonds) and eighth-oz (isolate). Store everything else inside Mylar sandwich bags. Design them to resemble old-fashioned fold-tops with seals, not zippers. Charge customers 100% markups.

# Cannabis Smallholdings

## Masterplan

**Agricultural Estates:**

According to TAX TREES, there shall be farming estates beyond city and town limits. The first generation of natives partaking in Operation White Wolf, named after a WWII plan, become the countries' future upper class. They provide affordable, 100% organic food while undercutting nonnatives' portions and prices with the double-grazing method! Moreover, not requiring subsidization reduces government deficits.

**Local Incorporations:**

For population counts, townships are 3A (school-district size) commuters (2k-4k), 4A markets (4k-8k) and 5A (8k-16k) satellites. Areas devoid of cities make a satellite their "de facto" city. City sizes vary from small micropolitans (16k-64k), solid metropolitans (64k-256k) and giant megalopolitans (256k-1.024mil). Urban definitions: Proper (city limits), parish (outskirts), municipality (both zones) and "tan" (ex: Greater Houston Area). Rural vocabulary: Town (limits), shire (outskirts) and civil township (both zones).

**Largeholdings:**

Plantations are professional agricultural estates exceeding 50 acres sandwiched halfway between outskirts and park systems, the latter privatized co-ops managed by deputy ranges. Plot sizes: Megas (50 acres), metros (100 acres), micros (200 acres), satellites (500 acres), markets (1,000 acres) and commuters (2,000 acres). Tenant farmers can lease sections for themselves, but plots cannot be subdivided due to future zoning laws. Smaller homesteads fall under the category of smallholdings. Permits should allow either to set aside up to 200 acres towards cannabis production.

## Smallholders

**Semi-professional:**

With marijuana and other future medicinal farms, these smallholdings shall become full-fledged, unsubsidized, professional farms! Hydroponic nutrients and additives (acids, bases peroxide) are considered 100% organic. Smallholding categories: Semi-pro (between 15-45 acres) hobby (5-15 acres), sustenance/tenant (1-4 acres) farms.

**Permitted Plots:**

Medical (5-acre), Delta-8 (10-acre), CBD-rich (20-acre), grain (50-acre), hybrid (100-acre) and fiber (200-acre) plots. Fields subdivide into two sections and one barn.

## Dro Barns

**Hydroponic Weed:**

Combine chains of bubbleponics buckets dubbed the Dutch bucket method. A reciprocating deep-water culture (RDWC) feed underwater roots while drip lines soak their growing medium: Pumice rocks! For rockwool (rock fiber), soak virgin plugs (cloning), cubes (germination) blocks (ornamentals) and slabs (ruderalis) in acidic water (pH 4.0) for at least 30 minutes, preferably overnight, to achieve a pH of 6.0.

**Aeroponic Nurseries:**

Incubators sprout seeds. Ultrasonic foggers cradle clone cutting covered by humidity domes. POS systems spray seedlings under low pressure and saplings high pressure. Barns need a storage silo, processing shed and carport. Operate surveillance drones.

## Crop Fields

**Compound Divisions:**

Split fields 90:10 between outer and inner blocks. Each one has its own nursery. A block has 2-5 patches organized by species and breeding programs. Crusher run roads provide access. Patch subsections demand processing sheds. Their glass greenhouses cultivate strains accommodated by 2ft-wide service aisles between individual rows.

**Complex Designs:**

Nurseries receive an awning for go-karts, storage silo and compost shed. Flood trays germinate sprouts while raceways cradle seedlings. Saplings are transplanted in peat pots. A block's hub houses its irrigation closet. Install micro sprinklers across inner blocks and macro-drip lines buried along outer areas. Set pH to 6-7 by adding sulfur.

**HIGH-LOW Strategy:**

Inner blocks employ shallow water culture (SWC) trays, nutrient film technique (NFT) raceways and active drip lines. Fill pots with mixtures of compost, ground pine needles, manure and recycled glass aggregate. Outer regions rely on ebb and flow (flooding/draining), Kratky (basket over water) buckets and wick systems. Potting soil is peat moss, alfalfa meal, vermicompost (compost/worms) and vermiculite (rocks). Ornamental potting mixes have coir (husks), potash (minerals), vermiculture (worm castings) and perlite (foam). Give both mycorrhizal fungi and beneficial nematodes.

**Shelterbelt Systems:**

All farms have greenbelts (wooded borders) serving as windbreaks to prevent future dust bowls. Study my first book, *Saving the United States*, and its forestry models. Slash-and-burn all perimeter vegetation. The Great Plains Shelterbelt replaces their belts with oak savannas! The Great Plains relies on American bamboo/canebrakes and was originally supposed to be treeless. Seasonal, prescribed burns enrich soil.

# Agricultural Practices

## Hemp Variants

**Industrial Subvariants:**

Fiber, hybrid hemp and grain plots lack hydroponic labs, nurseries and mixing sheds. Segregation in blocks and patches is unnecessary. Tractors plow, till, sow and reap everything. A plantation has at least two fields allowing one to rest between seasons.

**CBD-rich Variant:**

Inner blocks divide into three patches: Flash-frozen, slow-dried and breeding plants. Harvesting techniques will be discussed in further detail in the following section. Outer blocks operate like the plots above and ship dried product to CBD refineries. They're responsible for producing skin care products and orally-ingested herbal remedies. Dro barns generate dried flower without the intention of drug labs adding any D8 isolate.

## Marijuana Plots

**Medical/Recreational:**

Fields plant regular (soil-grown, regular) landraces. Outer regions tackle AA- flower (lower mids) for hash oil production. Inner blocks provide AA+ (upper mids) bud converted to goods such as kif (unpressed trichomes), hashish (refined trichomes) and charas (rolled resin). Dro barns craft indo nuggets from crossbreeds. Rude is A-grade (singles) quality only suitable for making flash-frozen extracts in CBN gummies.

**Tax, Title, License:**

Permit categories include CBD/CBN, Delta-8-sourced THCs, medical and recreational marijuana. Make states grant holders the right to establish an unlimited amount of plots/farms in their state. Breed medical phenotypes who's profiles are rich in minor cannabinoids for therapeutic effects. Match them with strains already loaded with their own parent molecules. For example: CBGA is the primordial version of CBG, etc.

**Derivatives of THCA:**

Tetrahydrocannabinolic acid (THCA). Organic THC: Tetrahydrocannabiphorol (THCP) > Tetrahydrocannabihexol (THCH) < Tetrahydrocannabutol (THCB) > Delta-9 (D9), Delta-8 (D8) > Tetrahydrocannabivarin (THCV). Synthetic: Tetrahydrocannabioctyl (THCjd) > Tetrahydrocannabinol acetate (THCO) > Tetrahydrocannabinol-Methoxy (THCM) > Hexahydrocannabinol (HHC) > Delta-10 (D10) > Delta-11 (D11). Edibles cause our livers to produce 11-hydroxy THC and it's way stronger than Hydrox4phc (PHC)!

# Cultivation Techniques

## Germination

### Ideal Incubation:

Set nurseries' humidity to 70%. Moisture helps seed casings sluff off. Wait until germs shrivel and fall off on their own. Some plants are kept as mother plants just for the sake of producing clones. Slice stems of cuttings diagonally underwater, dip them in rooting gel, stick in rockwool plugs and trim ends off leaves to reduce transpiration.

### LED Lighting:

LEDs: 300-watt (sprouts, 12"), 600-watt (seedlings, 18"), 1,000-watt (saplings, 24"), 2,000-watt (rude, 30") and 4,000-watt (adult, 36"). Colors: Seedlings/re-vegging (full-spectrum), veg (blue) and flowering (red). Hours: Re-vegging (24/0), seedlings/clones (20/4), autos (18/6), indoor (16/8), outdoor (14/10) and flowering (12/12). Add UV-B lighting during flowering to boost THC. UV-C wands eliminate pests and pathogens.

### Sea of Green:

String checkerboard netting above plants and tuck colas (stalks) underneath. Private reserves are grown in bubbleponics totes and given the screen of green (SCROG) treatment. To mainline, top above the third node and bend new growth horizontally. Oscillating fans improve air circulation and subwoofer vibrations strengthen stems.

### Feeding/Watering:

Follow directions on bags of organic additives. Some strains need more of one type of nutrient than others, so do research beforehand. During flowering, ingredients and portions differ. Leaf diagnosis: Curling (overwatered), limp (dry), yellow (starving), speckled (overfed), bleached tips (light burn), canoed (hot) and stunted (root-bound).

## Maturation

### Main Sequencing:

Fimm the top half of a plant's third node to create 3-5x as many colas. After two weeks, super top those and let rest for two more. Lollipop 1/3$^{rd}$ of underbrush away one week before running 12/12. Don't pour bong water on them or smoke nearby!

### PH/Humidity:

Reduce humidity by 5% every week during flowering until labs hit 40%. You'll need a humidifier and dehumidifier to do so. For pH ranges, hydro is 6.0 and regular 6.5.

# Flowering

**Defoliation Periods:**

Schwazz fan leaves off, but leave a few at the tops of each cola on day one. Do this again three weeks later. Monster crop the bottom $1/3^{rd}$ on week six to create more clones re-vegged under 24/0 lighting so you don't have to rely on mother plants anymore. During week nine, perform a flush for two weeks without feeding the plant. Doing so prevents headaches and foul aftertastes. Fan leaves may look bad, but that's normal. Harvest by week 11. This keeps sativa energizing, gives balanced hybrids their head high and makes indica/rude relaxing. Autoflowers like ruderalis take less time.

**Amber Alert System:**

Trichomes are visible under a jeweler's loupe and change color three times: Clear and dewy, white and cloudy, and golden amber. These crystals continue to mature during drying and curing. Hashish continues aging for many years! Harvest sativa 1:1 clear/white, balanced hybrids completely white and indica/ruderalis 1:1 white/gold.

**Grapes of Wrath:**

Anytime you see "grapes" on a plant, it's a male. If pistils are also present alongside those pollen sacks, you have a hermaphrodite (hermie or nanner) – ditch those ASAP!

# Harvesting

**Wet Trimming:**

The following four items are kept separate, wet-trimmed by machines and flash-frozen: Outer regular, indo popcorn nuggets, indo trim (sugar leaves/shake) and rude. Compost fan leaves and branches. Photo dependent stumps regrow after harvests.

**Slow-dry Method:**

Dry flower in rooms set to 60-70°F and 45-60% humidity. Hang plants upside-down on a rack for two weeks. Trim finished nuggets or mold off daily. If bud turns brown, it's too dry! Large stems should remain flexible while small ones become snappable. Scrape scissor hash off sheers. Drug labs convert these products into various extracts.

**Trimming/Deseeding:**

Dro is hand-trimmed and tweezed free of sugar leaves. Inner regular is machine-trimmed. Remove seeds from breeder plants and sell banks feminized/regular stock.

**Collection/Curing:**

Organize 11 piles: Deseeded dro, SCROG, SOG, indo popcorn, indo trim, rude, inner regular, inner popcorn, inner trim, outer and scissor hash. Cut colas down and stuff pounds in one-gallon jars filled ¾ full. One elbow is 448 g, not 454. Some semi trailers and boxcars on trains have refrigerators/freezers. Curing is performed in drug labs.

# Review

## Farm-to-Market

**Diverse Melting Pots:**

Co-ops host semestral meetings discussing trending strains, maintaining diversity by retaining old-school classics and showcasing traditional landrace extracts. Doing so prevents shortages and waste helping to stabilize the market. There are nearly 800 strains of cannabis and no single smallholding can cultivate all of them at once. Therefore, growers will be encouraged to sow different strains than their neighbors.

**Cannabis Rotations:**

Fiber can be harvested up to five times a year, hybrid hemp quarterly and grain every trimester. Sowing them tighter leads to greater yields. The same can be said about CBD-rich strains. Medical and recreational marijuana is usually semestral in nature.

**Accidental Innovation:**

Polyester is inferior to hemp. Cotton makes the best socks and underwear. Grain produces excellent supplements catering to those who are allergic to certain animal products. It's superior to soy protein powder in every way, but nothing beats whey!

## Hydroton

**Earth's Medium:**

Tobacco plantations also have a barn using my Dutch bucket/bubbleponics combo for shisha in hookahs. Unlike dro's fresh, crisp flavors generated from rocks, tobacco leaves have rich, earthy flavors. Therefore, large Hydroton (clay pebbles) is better. For sustenance, some potheads grow pot in a pot filled with tiny, clay pottery pieces!

**International Clay:**

Medical smallholdings growing various plants for prescription medications across the globe require Hydroton for their systems. Hydroponic mushrooms lack roots and instead have mycelium. Yet, spraying substrate over these pebbles works just fine.

# CHAPTER TWO
## *Legendary Strains*

### Quadrant 1:2

*Listed below is this chapter's section directory. Topics are grouped together in subsections and verses mark any further subdivision of information.*

*Overview* ............................................................................. 20

*Indica Hybrids* ..................................................................... 21

*Balanced Hybrids* ................................................................ 22

*Sativa Hybrids* ..................................................................... 23

*Top Landraces* ....................................................................24

*Autoflowers* ......................................................................... 25

*Review* .................................................................................. 26

# Overview

## Heritage

**Demographics:**

Marijuana is the most widely-used drug on the planet and it spawned diverse cultures breeding their own unique varieties. There are almost 800 strains, 500 hybrids, 200 crossbreeds and 100 natural landraces on Earth! No other genus in history has been bred like cannabis by mankind. Listed below are regions accredited for our strains.

**Emerald Triangle:**

Four regions in the U.S. are pioneering most of today's hybrids. Hawaii gave rise to Maui Wowie, the first to push THC levels to where they are now. And, that was in the '70s! The West Coast's ambassador is California. Three counties in NorCal nicknamed the Emerald Triangle from growing pot made balanced hybrids popular. Colorado represents the Rockies. The North constitutes a fourth region. The Netherlands is the biggest 420-friendly country in Europe. Britain's guerilla growers bred strains too.

## Vanguard

**Memory Lane:**

Before practicing hands-on crop planting, study the history of your regional strains. This includes today's contemporaries (2000s+), classics (1980s-1990s), old-school varieties surfers encountered in Hawaii, Jamaica, Africa and Indonesia (1970s-1980s), and traditional landraces discovered along the Hippie Hashish Trail (1950s-1960s).

**THC Percentages:**

Many hybrids were named after landraces and one phenotype (F#) could be a different species. For example: White Widow Auto is an indica, not a balanced hybrid. All THC percentages listed in this chapter are for Delta-9 content in hydroponically-grown nuggets. Regular flower is guaranteed to be lower before processing. After their concentrates are extracted, their numbers exceed those found in dro. I didn't include totals for the other types of THC found in cannabis because they're so low.

# Indica Hybrids

## Chillin'

**Killer Kine' Bud:**

Pre-98 Bubba Kush sets the bar for proper indica. It delivers CBN to insomniacs. Unfortunately, it can create "couch-lock", slowing you down. To counterbalance brain fog, add stupendous amounts of CBC. Cannabimovone (CBM) gives us the munchies. Cannabipinol (CBP) is therapeutic and most people refer to it as cannabicyclol (CBL).

**Kush Coma:**

The ideal minimum sedation should match Strawberry Sour D8 gummies by Cake. For vapes, try Mellow Monkey's Rare line of Raspberry Kush Indica (THCjd/HHC/CBN).

## Strains

**Photo-dependent:** Alphabetized

Big Bud: 85/15, 23-25% THC
Blueberry: 80/20, 16-24% THC
Bubba Kush: 80/20, 14-25% THC
Bubblegum: 60/40, 18-22% THC
Cheesecake: 70/30, 15-23% THC
Chemdawg: 55/45, 15-25% THC
Critical Kush: 90/10, 14-25% THC
G-13: 70/30, 22-29% THC
Garlic Cookies: 90/10, 21-25% THC
Gelato #45: 55/45, 23-26% THC
Girl Scout Cookies: 60/40, 20-28% THC
GMO Crasher: 70/30, 26-29% THC
Godfather OG: 60/40, 22-30% THC
Gorilla Glue: 60/40, 25-28% THC
Granddaddy Grape Ape: 70/30, 20% THC
Grandmaster Kush: 80/20, 18-28% THC
Gushers: 60/40, 15-25% THC
Headband: 60/40, 20-27% THC
Khalifa Kush: 80/20, 24-27% THC
Kosher Kush: 90/10, 22-25% THC
LA Confidential: 90/10, 20-26% THC
Northern Lights: 95/5, 16-26% THC
OG Kush: 75/25, 19-24% THC
Purple Punch: 80/20, 18-20% THC
Purple Urkle: 70/30, 18-21% THC
Sherbet: 85/15, 14-19% THC
Super Skunk: 65/35, 19-28% THC
UK Cheese: 80/20, 20-23% THC
Wedding Cake: 80/20, 20-24% THC
Wedding Crasher: 60/40, 17-21% THC
White Rhino: 80/20, 18-22% THC
Zkittlez: 70/30, 13-15% THC

# Balanced Hybrids

## Mellow

**Sticky Icky:**

Chronic was the gold standard of what a balanced hybrid should be until it passed the torch to White Widow. CBG increases creativity without making someone too hyperactive or exhausted. Cannabivarin (CBV) improves mental health and nerve function. Pre-rolls containing even hybrids are labelled as hybrid. Manufacturers mixing two or more different species together produce what's called a house blend.

**Creeper Weed:**

Imbalanced hybrids are already listed under their dominant species' category (indica, sativa, etc.). Even hybrids adopt the default term hybrid in most stores. Moreover, it needs to creep up on users like Stoney Patch hybrid gummies do. For vapes, effects should feel like Lemon Cookie Hybrid (THCP/HHC/D8/D10) Dome Wreckers by Work.

## Strains

**Photo-dependent:** Alphabetized

$100 OG: 50/50, 24% THC

Blackberry: 50/50, 26% THC

Buddha Tahoe: 50/50, 16-22% THC

Champagne Kush: 50/50, 26% THC

Cheetah Piss: 50/50, 16-22% THC

Chronic: 50/50, 20-22% THC

Chiquita Banana: 50/50, 30-34% THC

Glueberry OG: 50/50, 17-25% THC

Green Line OG: 50/50, 20-29% THC

Hawaiian Haze: 50/50, 26% THC

High School Sweetheart: 50/50, 23% THC

Ice: 50/50, 20% THC

Kryptochronic: 50/50, 17-25% THC

Larry OG: 50/50, 22-26%+ THC

Lemon Cookies: 50/50, 28% THC

MAC-1: 50/50, 20-23% THC

Purple Trainwreck: 50/50, 23% THC

Royal Gorilla: 50/50, 22-24% THC

Runtz: 50/50, 19-29% THC

Shark OG: 50/50, 22-27% THC

Skunk XL: 50/50, 17% THC

Skywalker: 50/50, 15-23% THC

Space Queen: 50/50, 16-23% THC

Sour OG: 50/50, 17-22% THC

Sundae Driver: 50/50, 14-16% THC

Venom OG: 50/50, 17-27% THC

White Russian: 50/50, 19-25% THC

White Widow: 50/50, 18-25% THC

# Sativa Hybrids

## Wild

**Straight Fire:**

Super Silver Haze is a Dutch gem, itself an offshoot of the original Neville's Haze. CBD leads to an outbreak of the "laughies" and boosts energy levels leading to more productivity during physical activities. Cannabinodivarin (CBVD) is excellent during rehabilitation training. Sativa's CBG creates better head highs than balanced hybrids.

**Furious Nugs:**

Gummies should feel like Cherry Garcia by A Gift From Nature. Combining properly-cured trichomes makes sativa your top-seller followed by even hybrids. Never let anything exceed the head high from Island Colada (D8/D10/CBD) by Sticky Greens!

## Strains

**Photo-dependent:** Alphabetized

Alaskan Thunderfuck: 70/30, 23% THC

AK-47: 65/35, 16-21.5% THC

Amnesia Haze: 80/20, 20% THC

Blue Dream: 60/40, 17-24% THC

Bruce Banner: 60/40, 24-29% THC

Chocolope: 95/5, 18-23% THC

Cinderella 99: 85/15, 16-22% THC

Ghost Train Haze: 80/20, 27% THC

Golden Tangie: 70/30, 25-27% THC

Green Crack: 65/35, 15-24% THC

Hawaiian Snow: 90/10, 18-24% THC

Head Cheese: 85/15, 19-28% THC

Hulkberry: 65/35, 27% THC

Jack Herer: 55/45, 15-24% THC

Kali Mist: 90/10, 12-22% THC

Laughing Budda: 75/25, 18-22% THC

Mimosa: 70/30, 17-27 THC

Lemon Cake: 70/30, 19-23% THC

Lemon Skunk: 60/40, 14-22% THC

Moby Dick: 75/25, 21% THC

Neville's Haze: 75/25, 15-23% THC

NYC Diesel: 60/40, 18-24% THC

Pineapple Express: 60/40, 18-25% THC

Purple Haze: 85/15, 14-19% THC

Sour Diesel: 90/10, 19-26% THC

Sour Dubble: 60/40, 16-26% THC

Strawberry Cough: 80/20, 22-26% THC

Super Lemon Haze: 80/20, 17-25% THC

Super Silver Haze: 80/20, 18-23% THC

Trainwreck: 80/20, 18-25% THC

# Top Landraces

## Ruderalis/Indica

**Ruderalis Purebreds:** Bonsai/Breeders

Kazakh: Kazakhstan, 10-15% THC

Siberian Standard: Russia, ≤ 1% THC

**Indica Purebreds:** Alphabetized

Afghani: Afghanistan, 17-22% THC

Balkhi: Afghanistan, 14-24% THC

Black Sea: Turkey, N/A

Chitral Kush: Pakistan, 21% THC

Hindu Kush: Pakistan, 14-22% THC

Ketama: Morocco, 14-17% THC

Lebanese Red: Lebanon, 12-25% THC

Mag: Iran, 19-23%+ THC

Mazar-i-Sharif: Afghanistan, 20% THC

Razavi Khorasan: Iran, 20% THC

Shirin Gol: Tajikistan, N/A

Sinai: Egypt, 15% THC

Syrian: Syria, N/A

Yangiyul: Uzbekistan, N/A

## Sativa/Hemp

**Sativa Purebreds:** Alphabetized

Acapulco Gold: Mexico, 19-23% THC

Bhutanese White: Bhutan, 11-15% THC

Ciskei: South Africa, 18-20% THC

Columbian Gold: Columbia, 14-20% THC

Chocolate Thai: Thailand, 12-16% THC

Congolese: Congo, 18-20% THC

Durban Poison: South Africa, 17-22% THC

Highland Lao: Laos, 13-22% THC

Kalamata Red: Greece, 12-20% THC

Kerala Gold: India, 14-18% THC

Kilimanjaro: Kenya, 11-20% THC

Kwazulu: South Africa, 17-20% THC

Kumaoni: China, 14-19% THC

Lamb's Bread: Jamaica, 17% THC

Malana Cream: India, 10-25% THC

Malawi Gold: Malawi, 14-18% THC

Mango Thai: Thailand, 18-22% THC

Manipuri: Myanmar, N/A

Maui Wowie: Hawaii, 17-26% THC

Nepalese: Nepal, 14-17% THC

Oaxaca Gold: Mexico, 12-23% THC

Parvati: India, 15-20% THC

Panama Red: Panama, 10-16% THC

Sinaloa Jarilla: Mexico, 12-15% THC

Swazi Gold: Swaziland, 14-18% THC

Vietnam Black: Vietnam, 25% THC

# Autoflowers

## Homegrown

**Personal Stashes:**

Autos prefer low stress training (LST) when they're seedlings. Bend tops horizontally to encourage node to orient themselves vertically. Once the horizontal branches on these saplings become too long, snap them without tearing their skin and position them vertically. This high stress training (HST) technique is called super cropping!

## Strains

**Ruderalis-dominated:** Medical-grade

Shiskaquine: ≤ 1% THC (Child Patients)

**Indica-dominated:** Alphabetized

| | |
|---|---|
| Blueberry Auto: 14% THC | Northern Lights Auto: 14% THC |
| Bubba Kush Auto: 17-21% THC | OG Kush Auto: 17-23% THC |
| Cheese Auto: 9-12% THC | Royal Critical Auto: 14% THC |
| Gelato Auto: 22% THC | Runtz Auto: 24-26% THC |
| Godfather OG Auto: 25% THC | Sherbet Auto: 16-20% THC |
| Gorilla Glue Auto: 24-26% THC | Skunk #1 Auto: 10-15% THC |
| GSC Auto: 20% THC | Wedding Cake Auto: 17-19% THC |
| Gushers Auto: 22% THC | White Widow Auto: 12-20% THC |
| Mazar Auto: 20% THC | Zkittlez Auto: 23% THC |

**Sativa-dominated:** Alphabetized

| | |
|---|---|
| Amnesia Haze Auto: 21% THC | Jack Herer Auto: 16% THC |
| AK-47 Auto: 20-25% THC | Mimosa Auto: 21% THC |
| Blue Dream Auto: 13% THC | Moby Dick XXL: 18% THC |
| Bruce Banner Auto: 25% THC | Pineapple Punch Auto: 20% THC |
| Cinderella Auto: 23% THC | Purple Haze Auto: 14-17% THC |
| Green Crack Auto: 24% THC | Sour Diesel Auto: 21% THC |
| Green Gelato Auto: 24% THC | Trainwreck Auto: 19% THC |

# Review

## Genetics

### White Labeling:

Never buy from white label companies! Their autos rarely achieve more than a 50% germination rate, grow slowly, flower prematurely and fail to properly branch out from their nodes. Photo varieties don't clone properly either. Pollen chucker is slang for mid-tier and its only good for beginners practicing. Quality breeders are several times more expensive, but whatever you do cultivate survives anything! Whomever decides to invest in costly F1s, God forbid inbred lines, should stick with these guys.

### Early Birds:

Fast flowering sativa and early flowering indica varieties come in handy. Apart from summer providing 14 hrs. of sunlight, most seasons offer 12. Climate-controlled, glass greenhouses with supplementary lighting let farmers achieve 3-4 harvests annually.

### Rude Awakening:

Autos require a minimum of 5-10% ruderalis, but anything exceeding 10-20% flowers to early. One benefit they have is not requiring 12/12 lighting during flowering, which leads to monstrous yields. It's advantageous in the tropics, a region prohibited to 1-2 semestral photo grows. Homegrown enthusiasts can place an ornamental rude in potting mix, atop a table. They massage live nectar off them to christen their weed!

## Breeding

### Next Generation:

Landraces are the hardiest strains with the most terpenes. What they lack in THC is compensated by their entourage effect, which is almost psychedelic in nature. However, hybrids still rule when it comes to dro production and homegrown applications due to their superior flower output. Landraces also contain the most minor cannabinoids. Breed better generations to create more affordable marijuana isolates and flavor additives to disposable or interchangeable vaporizer cartridges.

# CHAPTER THREE
## *Competitive Cannabis*

### Quadrant 1:3

*Listed below is this chapter's section directory. Topics are grouped together in subsections labeled by underlined bullets. Any further subdivision of information is organized into verses marked by bolded bullets.*

| | |
|---|---|
| *Overview* | 28 |
| *Persian Hashish* | 29 |
| *Himalayan Charas* | 30 |
| *Oriental Honey* | 31 |
| *Review* | 32 |

# Overview

## New World

**Perfect Pedigrees:**

Most of the nearly 800 aforementioned strains were only popular for a few years at best before being discarded by another one. Trends seek to be appealing, not achieve lasting quality. There are way too many to begin with! So, avoid following foolish bandwagons, but keep an eye out for contemporaries that are legends in the making. Moonrocks are caviar nuggets dipped in hash oil and coated by kif (loose trichomes).

**Phenomenal Phenomics:**

Whenever an F1 hybrid is bred from two existing crossbreeds, genetic diversity shrinks. Once they create an inbred of an inbred from it, you can't go any further than an F5 without experiencing mutations and defects. What breeders can do is perfect new phenotypes of existing strains, especially when it comes to medical marijuana.

**Landrace Initiatives:**

By spreading awareness on a global scale, we can educate cannabis cultivators how hybrids and landraces must work together! Without crossbreeds, how could the Middle East's dro win future Cannabis Cups? Are people aware converting stale bud into dabs and hash reduces waste? Strains rated as singles (A-grade) can undergo terpene extraction in drug labs to give disposable CBD vapes their amazing flavors.

## Old World

**Traditions of the Trade:**

Bud (flower) is covered in crystals (trichomes) and pistils (hairs). Loose trichomes (kif) are sold in dispensaries, refined to make hashish (pressed kif) or unpressed bubble hash (refined kif). Bubble hash can be soft-pressed, doing so turns it into bricks. Kief (kif/tobacco mixture) is popular European cigarettes. Keef is anything miscellaneous, such as the powder collected underneath grinders or kif adhered to moonrocks that's no longer loose. Nectar is rubbed off colas (stalks) to produce charas (rolled resin).

# Persian Hashish

## Kif Farms

**Land of Kush:**

Indica is named after the Indian Hindu Kush mountains. I hypothesize two things: First, its spread to the Durand Line through the Wakhan Corridor bordering Western China. Second, a massive extinction of undiscovered landraces between Egypt and Morocco along North Africa's Mediterranean coastline. Mankind's irresponsibility led to Saharan prairies' desertification. Islamic countries bordering Afghanistan eradicated existing stands in their region. Ruderalis overtook Khazakstan and Siberia.

**Afghani Action:**

Scrape scissor hash off sheers to produce flower rosin (1-star) gummies. Rubbing finger hash from gloves yields hash rosin (2-star) cannabutter. Lay crystals over parchment in a tray. Heat a stove, add tea for pliability and roll them flat with a rod.

## Dry Sift

**Moroccan Method:**

Flower is dried in a dark cellar for two months. Layer three screens over of drum and cover colas before spanking. By now, bud is brittle enough to shatter upon impact releasing even the trichomes inside their cores. Periodically empty these bowls and repeat until there's no sift left to scrape through. Tap containers to prevent kif from sticking along their sides. Most will be pressed into bricks of hashish, some sold as is.

**Oh, Hashish Please:**

Store kif in half-gallon jars and bury it underground to age. Give blondes (early harvest) three months, browns (yellow, ripe) six and darks (black/red, late) 12. Pollen presses fabricate bricks of hashish. For blocks, give dry-sift glossy, hard-pressed exteriors and bubble hash matte, soft-pressed finishes. Apply gold/red-colored seals before chopping. Slice blocks down to gram-sized cubes stored in half-gallon jars. Always present one reassembled slab on display to attract attention from customers.

**Sands of Time:**

Inventory could easily spend 2-5 years changing hands between suppliers and sitting on shelves waiting for potential customers. By the time someone buys the last jar and finishes it, their last nug is aged to perfection never exceeding 8-10. There are stories of bricks lasting nearly 50! However, quality slowly diminishes after 12-year mark.

# Himalayan Charas

## Resin Farms

**Nectar of the Gods:**

High humidity levels in the Himalayas prevented laborers from properly sieving kif off dead plants. Instead, the Indians, Tibetans, Nepalese and Bhutanese people decided to rub nectar off living plants as an alternative. This practice dates back to 2,000 BC. Before the crackdown of '76, Malana, Kashmir and Kathmandu led the way in resin.

**Five-finger Discount:**

Set aside any spent plant material below as your scissor hash. Developing countries rely on rolling pins to press flower rosin (1-star) to create gummies. Rub finger hash off gloves to produce hash rosin (2-stars). Add that to butter to make cannabutter.

## Essence

**Hand Pressing:**

During flowering, farmhands slide their hands over stalks to strip all the flowers and leaves off plants. Continue rolling them around until no more resin can be extracted. Color is determined by how early one harvests a plant. Gold means early, brown standard timing and black late. Roll this resin into fingers, tosh balls and temple balls.

**Sicca Weights:**

One-gram fingers are popular amongst Rastafarians in Jamaica! Indians love tosh balls. A tola of hash is only 10 grams, not 12. Temple balls used to be a common occurrence in Tibet before China enacted prohibition. Some were an entire ounce!

**Fresh Fragrance:**

Unlike modern charas, they contain fresh plant material. Authentic Indian charas are rich in terpenes, which add flavor. Whenever tokers smoke them, they interact with other cannabinoids to induce a greater high. That's called the entourage effect. Drying takes two weeks. For aging, follow the same 3-6-12 month rule from earlier.

## Melt Ratings

**Half-melt:** "Fingers." Temple (4-star) and tosh (3-star) balls.

**Food Grade:** "Bhang." Cannabutter (2-star) and gummies (1-star).

# Oriental Honey

## Honey Oil

**Comfort Food:**

Cannabis was first discovered in the Altai Mountains 12,000 years ago. Emperor Shen Nung, regarded as the father of Chinese medicine, started using this herb in 2,800 BC. India incorporated crushed weed in their food and beverages around 2,000 BC. Indians pioneered infused vegetable oil by dissolving charas during the 19$^{th}$ century.

**Chemical X:**

Butane honey oil (BHO) relied on toxic solvents known to cause explosions in drug labs. Landrace initiatives teach cannabis chemists in developing countries how to extract hash oil without using petrochemicals and provide access to these resources.

**Secret Weapon:**

Steam distillation is crucial to the CBD industry. Without stills, they couldn't produce various grades of all-natural oils. These include skin care products, oral supplements and vapes. Grain hemp no longer relies on hexane to generate quality hemp seed oil.

## Concentrates

**Organic Alternatives:**

Concentrates listed below are organized from historic to most current. Many were solvent-based and obsolete. Subsequently, I won't go into detail discussing what they are or how they're created. Distillate must endure three transformations to exist.

**Under Pressure:**

Oil: Raw Crude > Refined Essential > Purified Distillate

Edibles: Finger Hash > Hash Rosin (2-star) > Cannabutter

Gummies: Scissor Hash > Flower Rosin (1-star) > Chewables

**Under the Gun:**

Diamonds: Shatter > Live Diamonds > Rosin Diamonds > Live Sugar

Wax: Budder (Butter) > Live Badder (Batter) > Crumble > Sugar Wax

Resin: Snap n' Pull (Taffy) > Live Resin > Live Sauce > Live Nectar

Rosin: Flower Rosin > Hash Rosin > Live Rosin > Live Sap

# Review

## Flower

**Straight As:**

<u>AAAAA</u>: Quins (moonrocks). Dip deseeded dro in live sap before rolling it in kif.

<u>AAAA</u>: Quads (private reserve). Cola tops from indoor, hydroponic, SCROG grows.

<u>AAA</u>: Trips (premium flower). Top-shelf colas off indoor, hydroponic, SOG setups.

<u>AA+</u>: Dubs (upper mids). Inner meadows. Crops are given potting mix/sprinklers.

<u>AA-</u>: Dubs (sub mids). Outer meadows. Strains utilizing potting soil/drip lines.

<u>A</u>: Singles (ruderalis). Indo dro for CBN gummies, breeding and ornamentals.

**B Section:**

<u>Popcorn (B)</u>: Nuggets set aside towards Piatella, champagne hash and charas.

<u>Shake (C)</u>: Loose flower bits. Mixed together with trim to produce scoopable kif.

<u>Trim (D)</u>: Crystallized sugar leaves. Don't include stripped fan leaves or stems!

## Hashish

**Melt Ratings:**

<u>Full-melt</u>: Leaves no ash and very little residue in the nails of dab rigs.

<u>Half-melt</u>: Produces clean, white ash. Perfect for hookahs and chillums!

<u>Food Grade</u>: Scissor and finger hash. Private reserve edibles get live rosin.

**Star System:**

<u>6-star</u>: Piatella and champagne hash. Hash oil dedicated to dabbing or vaping.

<u>5-star</u>: Static and dry-sift hashish. Requires static electricity or ultra-fine sieving.

<u>4-star</u>: Charas. Cold water (bubble hash) or hand-rolled (8hrs+ per ball/finger).

<u>3-star</u>: Kif. Cold-water extraction on sugar leaves or Moroccan Method's dry sift.

<u>2-star</u>: Cannabutter with hash rosin. Private reserve edibles contain live rosin.

<u>1-star</u>: Flower rosin gummies. Superior to essential oil or purified distillate.

# CHAPTER FOUR
## *Natural Medications*

### **Quadrant 1:4**

*Listed below is this chapter's section directory. Topics are grouped together in subsections labeled by underlined bullets. Any further subdivision of information is organized into verses marked by bolded bullets.*

*Overview* .................................................................................. 34

*Pharmaceutical Farms* .............................................................. 35

*Psychedelic Lodges* .................................................................. 36

*Hallucinogenic Plots* ................................................................ 37

*Review* ..................................................................................... 38

# Overview

## Medical Farms

**Pharmaceutical Plots:**

To win the drug war, convert the World's hard drugs into life-saving, non-intoxicating, prescription medication! Harvesting, drying and curing techniques determine which chemicals will be present. Continue the 90/10 block split utilized by cannabis fields. Refine crops and remove all intoxicating compounds to create 100% organic, broad-spectrum, gel caps! Drug labs can achieve an all-natural rating by converting isolates and designer synthetics to organic molecules found in nature. For $CO_2$ extractions, start with a subcritical pass followed by more intense supercritical ones afterwards.

## Hydric Fields

**Hydroton Mediums:**

Everything else comes in the form of a tablet pill made by pollen press, skin patch or resin packet. It's mostly leaves, bark, sap, roots, mushrooms and flowers. Hydroton gives them an earthiness that makes me think of soil hugging rockwool cubes. Outer nurseries get medium-sized pellets, inner zones small grains and hydro labs big balls.

**Rainforest Basins:**

Monsoons force farmers to unleash flood irrigation to reduce standing water in certain parts of their plots by moving it elsewhere. Outer blocks employ surface flooding while inner regions rely on subirrigation pumps to raise their water tables. This is a stark contrast to buried drip lines and micro sprinklers outside rainforests.

**Tropical Highlands:**

Cloud forests are almost as hydric (swampy), but prone to rolling terrain favoring traditional sprinkler systems over flood irrigation. Outer blocks install central-pivot systems. Inner blocks tow wheel-lines (lateral move unit) for superior performance compared to their outer zones. In areas where tractors run the risk of getting stuck in a rut, beasts of burden (oxen, mules, etc.) pull equipment across rougher terrain.

# Pharmaceutical Farms

## Sedatives

**Narcotic Dope Farms:**

Immature poppy pods are periodically scored with vertical cuts. Latex sap darkens as it congeals before being collected to create opiates (natural opioids). Chemists need to refine these compounds into non-intoxicating pain killers and muscle relaxers. Doing so prevents patients from developing addictions or experiencing withdrawals.

**Medical Marijuana:**

Many patients prioritized therapy over potency. Potting mixes kept THC levels down and achieved organic ratings. However, hydroponic systems now have access to 100% organic nutrients rendering this practice obsolete. Doing so makes medical marijuana more potent and prettier-looking than the best recreational-grade hydro!

## Nootropics

**Safrole Fields:**

Distilleries produce safrole oil and MDMA (refined ecstasy, aka molly) from crop fields. MDA (sally) is isolated from excess stocks. Sassafras (North America), Brazilian sassafras (Latin America) and star anise (temperate Asia) trees are excellent sources.

**Nutmeg Crops:**

Indonesian highlands are home to nutmeg, a tree rich in MMDA (euphoric drug). First, farmhands grind husks off the seeds' shells. Distillation is performed before isolation occurs. Eggnog and mace are two popular products sold in grocery stores.

## Stimulants

**Cocaine Fields:**

Pure snow can be extracted without toxic solvents. South American herders often chew coca leaves along mountain trails for energy. They're stronger than most pre-workout powder and energy drinks, so just stick to making non-psychoactive tablets!

**Khat Farming:**

Paralleling Latin America's blow is Khat. It grows in Ethiopian mountains and its leaves are also chewed by herders for the same reasons. Press the same kind of tablets.

# Psychedelic Lodges

## Funny Farms

### The Spirit Animals:

Throughout history, indigenous tribes have always operated sweat lodges. There, hallucinogens are given to those embarking on a vision quest. An experienced user who supervises sessions is called a trip sitter. To preserve this sacred tradition as a Sabbatarian Christian, do two things: First, convert everything to non-psychoactive prescription meds and sell it to fund the farms. Second, consume cannabis edibles to induce psychedelic trips: Run: THCB (beginners) > THCH (regulars) > THCP (experts).

### Behind the Stick:

Sitters walk beginners through their journey and stop bad trips with emergency CBD kits. They contain disposable vapes and essential oil bottles to alleviate any negative side effects. If stronger treatment is needed, switch to CBN. Lodges may continue offering actual hallucinogens, but should create custom kits to counteract their highs.

### Alice in Wonderland:

Regional cultivation: Amazonia (ayahuasca vines, sanango bushes), Central America (morning glory vines, salvia herbs), Andean (San Pedro/Peruvian torch cacti), Native America (peyote), Middle East (Syrian rue flowers, mandrake plants), Africa (kwashi flowers, acacia/iboga trees) and Oceania (screw pine). Magic mushrooms are native to all these regions. Turn this flora and fungi into non-inebriating pharmaceuticals!

## Medications

### Psychedelic Therapy:

Hallucinogens could be used to treat a variety of ailments ranging from severe drug addiction, arthritis, chronic bloating, major depression, mental health disorders, post-traumatic embitterment disorder (PTED), post-traumatic stress disorder (PTSD), skin conditions and sea sickness. Foundation grants and corporate funds geared towards psychedelic research could lead to new breakthroughs in modern medicine!

### Psychoactive Agents:

Here's a list of hallucinogens, found within each crop, from strongest to weakest: Scopolamine (borrachero, mandrake), ibogaine (Iboga, sanango), DMT (ayahuasca, acacia, screw pine), salvinorin A. (salvia), psilocbin (shrooms), mescaline (peyote, Peruvian torch, San-Pedro), harmaline/harmine (Syrian rue) and LSA (morning glory).

# Hallucinogenic Plots

## Mescaline Fields

**Vertical Farming Poles:**

Rainforests mandate the most wasteful forms of irrigation to avoid drowning. Outer blocks demand surface flooding and inner areas run subirrigation pumps. Steep mountains improvise central-pivots (outers) and towed wheel lines (inners). Arid climates need flow-drip emitters (outers) and microtubing (inners). For nurseries, vertical poles are entirely aeroponic; everyone else follows Chapter One's directions.

**Aeroponic Irrigation:**

Greenhouses and indoor tower gardens install commercial aeroponic systems. Therefore, they don't have growing mediums. However, transplant pots offer two quality grades of potting mixes: Outer and inner. Nurseries install ultrasonic foggers (germination), low-pressure units (seedlings) and high-pressure devices (saplings). These commercial modules house built-in monitor screens and proprietary software.

**Magic Mushrooms:**

Grow labs' aeroponic towers feature the World's first aeroponic mushrooms! Fungi lack roots. Instead, they have mycelium spores decomposing rotting material called substrate. As water from the mist evaporates, deposits develop over these spores. Sprayers are regulated by digital POS systems known as biological systems matrixes.

## Dual Extractions

**Quick Dry (Inner Block):**

First, remove cacti skins. Next, slice stalks ¼-inch thick and sun dry them for 2-3 days. Afterwards, chop pieces into curing jars for 4-7 days. Place everything in horizontal dryers with large caps in the back and small ones out front. Heat oven to 158°F and check batches every 1-2 hours. Then, let them cool. Cure for 1-2 days before creating distillates. At the end, laboratories process extracts into organic tablets for patients.

**$CO_2$ (Outer Block):**

Flash-freeze harvests collect in outer meadows. Run all crops, including dry-cured buttons, through a $CO_2$ machine to remove psychedelic ingredients and create broad-spectrum products. These items differ from full-spectrum goods designed to induce highs, such as recreational marijuana or D8 hemp, found in most smoke shops. Any remaining isolates will be refined by drug labs to manufacture all-natural tablets.

# Review

## Substances

### Drug Schedules:

Reorganize classifications by how dangerous the high is experienced, not by their addictiveness. Certain drugs in each category are equally deadly to each other. Let's make schedule I barbiturates (hypnotic), schedule II hallucinogens (psychedelic), schedule III nootropics (euphoric), schedule IV stimulants (uppers) and schedule V sedatives (downers)! Black-marketed substances shall be considered subcategories. Smugglers' legal punishments are based on drug types, quantities and prior offenses.

### Five Categories:

Barbiturates are hypnotic, hallucinogens induce hallucinations, nootropics euphoric, stimulants energizing and sedatives narcotic. Stimulants treat anxiety, improve concentration and reduce chronic weakness. Sedatives reduce physical pain, nausea, inflammation and sleep disorders. Nootropic therapy helps heal from past traumas. Higher categories, like barbiturates or hallucinogens, require more caution in their uses than stimulants or sedatives. Therefore, lists flow from most to least dangerous.

## Enforcement

### Digital Breathalyzers:

DWIs and public intoxication (PI) citations demand custom-designed breathalyzers, cotton swabs to collect mucus and saliva, and test results that take minutes, not hours. Heavy users' blood work often tests positive whenever they're sober. Urine results go back weeks, hair years and spinal taps lifetimes. So, don't depend on them!

### Drug Testing:

Urine results show weeks of prior use and is excellent for businesses. Amend laws so company drug tests won't discriminate against medical patients and policemen can't force blood work from citizens. Courtrooms rely on blood tests to reveal months of usage and plucking hair follicles to explore years of one's substance abuse history.

# CHAPTER FIVE
## *Factory Production*

### Quadrant 2:1

Listed below is this chapter's section directory. Topics are grouped together in subsections labeled by underlined bullets. Any further subdivision of information is organized into verses marked by bolded bullets.

*Overview* ............................................................................ 40

*Hemp Refineries* ................................................................ 41

*Hash Factories* .................................................................. 42

*Processing Plants* .............................................................. 43

*Review* ............................................................................... 44

# Overview

## General

**Factory Direct:**

Manufacturers can rebrand everything growers send them as their own products. Additionally, neither party is forbidden from performing transactions with other companies. This promotes healthy competition and higher industry standards. If a local farm or factory co-op is carteling quality down, simply switch to another one.

**Industrial Plazas:**

Most compounds need to be located within the industrial parks of major anchor cities. Property costs will be more affordable and freight trains can unload goods behind warehouses' garages. Forklifts load cargo pallets at train stations directly into complexes via garages. Foyers face public streets ready to greet potential clientele.

## Specific

**Triple Treatment:**

Divide complexes into seven zones: Cellar, press factory, processing plant, industrial kitchen, isolate laboratory and warehouse. Labs receive refined commodities from refinery sections. Kitchens cook cannabutter (THC-rich butter). Processing plants are stocked jars of concentrates while factory press rooms create kif, hashish and charas.

**Dry-cured Inner:**

Stash gallon jars in dim-lit cellars. Sativa needs four weeks, hybrids six and indica eight. Set humidity to 55-65% and temperature at 60-70°F. Amber-to-white trichome ratios: Rude 90/10, indica 80/20, hybrid 70/30, sativa 60/40 and CBD flower 50/50.

**Cold-cured Outer:**

Outer, rude, indo popcorn and indo trim are flash frozen. Then, two $CO_2$ passes isolate live (uncured) nectar (exterior) and sap (interior). Product is cold-cured in industrial refrigerators between 1-8 weeks. Once color lightens to a golden-amber, it's ready!

# Hemp Refineries

## Purification

**Industrial Mills:**

Textile mills process dried stalks from fiber to create alternatives to polyester used in clothing, shoe linings, canvas, blackout curtains and rope. Hemp seed separated from grain varieties produces vegan protein powder, hemp milk, granola, cereal mixes and vitamin supplements. Research labs extract isolates and terpenes from stripped bud.

**CBD Distilleries:**

Run portions of reggie collected from inner blocks through rosin presses to create flower rosin (1-star) gummies. Distill the majority into three oil grades. Raw oil excels in topical skin care items. Essential oil belongs in eye dropper bottles intended for oral consumption. Distillate enriched by natural terpenes is placed into vaporizers.

## Laboratories

**Double Extraction:**

Everything else comes from the outer regions' bud. Subcritical extractions precede supercritical passes. Convert most of your CBD into CBDV. Shoot for a 2:1 ratio of CBDV to CBD in bases. Other isolates are incorporated via solventless tinctures to achieve greater consistency over minor cannabinoid profiles. D8 vaporizers need diamonds, wax, resin and rosin. Be sure to freeze-dry and cold-cure said inventory.

**Broad-spectrum:**

Regions prohibiting recreational marijuana use are legally-required to source their cannabinoids exclusively from CBD-rich hemp strains. CBD/CBN products are already below 0.3% THC, but consumers want broad-spectrum products during drug tests.

**Delta-8 Production:**

Leftover D9 isolated by broad-spectrum production processes results is transformed into THCjd, THCO, THCM, HHC, D8 and D10. Excess CBD can also be converted too.

**Minor Profiles:**

CBD-rich phenotypes are listed as a strain's F# numbers and are bred to include more of the following cannabinoids. CBD becomes cannabidiphorol (CBDP), cannabidiol monomethylether (CBDM) and cannabidivarin (CBDV). CBG evolves into cannabidiol monomethylether (CBGM), cannabielsoin (CBE) and cannabivarin (CBV) over time.

# Hash Factories

## Extraction

**Static Sifting:**

The art of dry sifting is further refined by static electricity. To produce hash, strip inner colas (5-star hashish) and inner trim (3-star kif). Massage popcorn nuggets to create charas (4-star). Residue accumulating on gloves is called finger hash; save it for the next subsection. Salvage spent plant material to produce bubble hash (6-star).

**Cold Water:**

Micron screens become progressively finer in washers (220, 160, 120, 90, 73, 45, 25). Only pour ultra-purified, ice water (32-34°F) in when processing bubble hash. Save everything from the bottom three filters. Piatella hash requires indo popcorn and champagne is fed everything else. If hash is grey after freeze drying: Throw it away!

## Press Work

**Pollen Presses:**

Hard-pressed static kif yields glossy bricks extending shelf life. Soft-pressed bubble hash results in a matte-finished exterior and less damage to delicate trichome heads. Bricks should have cinnamon-colored shells and golden-amber interiors. Cured charas are hand-rolled into temple balls, tosh balls, or fingers prior to being polished.

**Rosin Expellers:**

Flower rosin (1-star) is pushed out of scissor hash to create gummies by rosin presses. Start at 180°F under 550 psi; go up from there. Finger hash collected off gloves becomes hash rosin (2-star) in cannabutter. Start at 140°F under 300 psi, then rise. Indo trim is freeze-dried and cold-cured to make live rosin (2-star), private reserve edibles. Dr. Zodiac and Kurupt, two West Coast rappers, invented moonrocks! Our sun rocks use live sap. Snowballs take it a step further by adding a layer of THCA powder. Deseeded dro is dunked in oil, caked with kif and left to set until hardened.

**Decarboxylation:**

Heat activates cannabinoids in cannabis. Eddies aren't smoked, so they must decarb ahead of time to unlock psychoactive properties. Place rosin in an oven set between 200-245°F for 30-45 minutes. Test potency before portioning. Gummies are 25-100 mg. Give each pound of cannabutter 2.4 g THC. D9 butter might contain up to 4 g of rosin. THCB, THCH and THCP varieties utilize isolate powder. So, math accordingly!

# Processing Plants

## Essentials

**Full Spectrum:**

D8 products cannot exceed 0.3% D9 and some states limit medical marijuana to 0.5% lozenges. However, medical and recreational marijuana in other regions isn't bound by this rule. All products are considered full-spectrum. Vaporizers need diamonds, wax, resin and rosin. Chapter Nine teaches you how to make them. Dab pens, nectar straws and dab rigs favor oil rich in high terpene extract (HTE), aka terp sauce. It boosts flavor and entourage effect. Shoot for a golden-amber color on concentrates.

**Vaping Cartridges:**

Bases are 2:1 CBDV/CBD (sativa), CBV/CBG (balanced) and CBC/CBN (indica). Ditto on these base-to-tincture ratios: 1.25 g (0.75 g/.5 g), 2.5 g (1.5 g/1 g) and 5 g (2.5 g/2 g).

**THC/CBN Gummies:**

Bake most of the rude oil until browned, isolate its CBN using the same extraction techniques from earlier, make it broad-spectrum and tincture (solventless version) it back into the remaining uncooked oil. Totals: CBD-rich hemp > 3 g of gelatin (300 mg, 1:1 ratio), THCV > 3 g (300 mg, 2:1), D8 > 4 g (300 mg, 4:1) and D9 > 5 g (300 mg, 8:1).

## Isolates

**CBN Tinctures:**

Without terpenes, isolates don't hit as hard. CBN totals, gummies: CBN (50 mg), THCV (50 mg), D8 (50 mg) and D9 (50 mg). CBN vaporizer (base-to-tincture) totals: 1.25 g small (0.75 g/.5 g), 2.5 g standard (1.5 g/1 g) and 5 g large (2.5 g/2 g) oil cartridges.

**Natural Crystalline:**

Technicians convert excess Delta-9 isolate to other forms of naturally-occurring THC, saving money. Vaping carts follow my 2:1 rule regardless of which type of THC is used. Here's each edible's total: For gummies, do THCV (25 mg), D8 (50 mg) and D9 (100 mg). Traditional edibles administer THCP (10 mg), THCH (20 mg) and THCB (40 mg).

**Entourage Effect:**

CBC degrades into cannabichromevarin (CBCV), cannabinol (CBN), cannabimovone (CBM) and cannabicylol (CBL). Future phenotypes are bred to include more of these minor cannabinoids and anything not mentioned that's narcotic (sleep-inducing).

# Review

## Standards

**Potency Levels:**

Regardless of what cannabinoid said cannabis is rich in, potencies need to fall within my specifications listed below. Legal Delta-9 limits in some states average $\leq$ 0.3%. CBN marijuana tops $\geq$ 0.2% and CBD hemp exceeds $\geq$ 0.1%. Just because a state allows recreational marijuana doesn't mean they support Delta-8. So, watch what you sell!

Crystalline: 90-100%

Live Sugar: 80-100%

Sugar Wax: 70-95%

Live Nectar: 60-95%

Live Sap: 50-90%

Temple Balls: 40-80%

Bubble Hash: 30-70%

Static Hash: 25-60%

Kif/Keef Crystals: 20-50%

Top-shelf Flower: 16-35%

Mid-level Flower: 10-16%

Popcorn/Shake: $\leq$ 10%

## Shipping

**Dank Inventory:**

Storage requires 55-65% humidity. Warehouses need 65-75°F temperatures and dim lighting around shelving to prevent potential oxidation. Otherwise, smell, taste, texture, color and quality quickly degrade. Although, aisles are given more ambient lighting than shelving racks to increase visibility. Some wholesalers lack access to railways. Therefore, it's important for you to set aside garage access for their semis.

**Four Horsemen:**

As previously mentioned, leave dro in its gallon-jars. Slice hash bars and roll charas down to the gram. Store them inside half-gallon jars. They don't have to be weighed afterwards and can be reassembled back into bricks within dispensary displays! Dabbing concentrates are portioned directly into quart jars. Vaporizers, eddies and paraphernalia are all boxed. Load all four onto cardboard trays atop wooden pallets wrapped with plastic. Thus, product post-cellar cannot be burped until it hits stores.

# CHAPTER SIX

## *Inventory Management*

### **Quadrant 2:2**

*Listed below is this chapter's section directory. Topics are grouped together in subsections labeled by underlined bullets. Any further subdivision of information is organized into verses marked by bolded bullets.*

Overview .................................................................................. 46

Distribution System ................................................................ 47

Industrial Units ........................................................................ 48

Homegrown ............................................................................. 49

Review ...................................................................................... 50

# Overview

## **Raised Bars**

**Cream of the Crop:**

Properly-flushed dro is devoid of excess nitrogen giving it its signature lime-green color. Quality nuggets are shrouded in cured trichomes, most of which aren't clear, brown or black. Red, purple, pink and blue colors are generated by flavonoids tied to plant genetics. Brown trichomes are deteriorating while black ones dead. Nothing moldy or soggy is allowed or else it's discarded. Sugar leaves should be tweezed off.

**Righteous Resin:**

Green hash is contaminated with plant matter. Although it's an acceptable color for customers' grinder keef, it doesn't meet dispensary standards for kif. Grey (after drying) is poorly-made bubble. White hashish has clear-colored grains with a white exterior. This is caused by immature trichomes, a byproduct of using unripe plants.

## **Honest Scales**

**Weights and Measurements:**

Pound: "Elbow." 448 grams = two half-pounds.

Half-pound: "Half-pack." 224 grams = two quarter-pounds.

Quarter-pound: "Q-P." 112 grams = two twin-ounces.

Two-ounce: "Double." 56 grams = two ounces.

Ounce: "Lid." 28 grams = two half-ounces.

Half-ounce: "Half-zip." 14 grams = two fourths.

Fourth: "Quad." 7 grams = two eighths.

Eighth: "Slice." 3.5 grams = two half-eighths.

Half-eighth: "Teenth" 1.75 grams = one blunt.

Gram: "Single." One gram = one cigarillo.

Half-gram: "Half-g." One half-g = one joint.

# Distribution System

## Shipping

**Online Orders:**

Bulk shipments for individuals are mailed to their door. Wholesalers supply parcels stuffed with duffle bags full of goods. Amend possession laws so there are no limits to how much someone can carry, store or grow. Retail packages contain tote bags filled with resealable Mylar bags shaped like bricks and quart jars containing dabs.

**Wholesale Shipments:**

Smaller, in-store purchases are placed in baggies and dab shots. Larger transactions feature smaller sacks shaped like sandwich bags – nostalgia! Retailers transfer bud to smaller mason jars. Serving containers also double as smelling jars. They showcase a boatload of merchandise and hold a lot of gas underneath their lids. Storage rooms house larger jars for restocking. Burn incense near the door, never around registers!

**Retail Purchases:**

Sold merchandise is tucked away in drawstring handbags. Customers are limited: Dro (double), hash (lid), oil (half-zip) and isolate (quad). Markups: 5% raw materials, 10% grower's, 20% manufacturer's, 40% wholesaler's and 100% retailer's rate. Undercut nonnatives until you reach my book's prices. Maintaining these figures prevents destabilizing the industry due to potential oversaturation within the market itself.

## Handling

**Bags of Weed:**

Unlike compressed brick weed, which completely ruins all flower quality, packs are superior! Elbows, half-packs and Q-Ps belong in gallon bags rubbed with isopropyl. Rub all other bags inside and out. Vacuum seal the next bag and stop the machine once the noise changes. Give the exterior one final wipe with bleach. Ounces, half-ounces and fourths are sacks. Eighths, half-eighths and gram baggies are called bags.

**Brick System:**

Large quantities of hash, namely Q-Ps and up, make bricks. Smaller amounts, doubles and down, form blocks. Marijuana is the only global product measured by the U.S. customary system. That's because our country is home to the Emerald Triangle (weed-growing region) of the World. However, medicinal opiate and stimulant farms utilize the metric system. Smaller portions were nicknamed 8-balls and kilos keys.

# Industrial Units

## Freighting

**Farm-to-market:** *Grower > Manufacturer*

Freight Boxcar: 100 tons max (boxes, glass paraphernalia)

Well Car: 100 tons max, 60-75 tons standard, (pallets of cannabis)

40ft Shipping Container: 33.6 tons max, 8.5 ft height (cannabis pallets)

20ft Shipping Container: 26.5 tons max, 8.5 ft height (paraphernalia)

Quad-axle Trailer: 40 tons max, 48,000 lbs standard, 14 ft height

Tri-axle Trailer: 30 tons max, 42,000 lbs standard, 14 ft height

Tandem Trailer: 22 tons max, 34,000 lbs standard, 14 ft height

Single-axle Trailer: 10.5 tons max, 20,000 lbs standard, 14 ft height

**Factory-direct:** *Manufacturer > Wholesaler*

Oversized-pallet: 1,250 kg max, 2,500 lbs standard, 7 ft height

Full-pallet: 1,000 kg max, 2,000 lbs standard, 6.5 ft height

Half-pallet: 500 kg max, 1,000 lbs standard, 3.5 ft height

Quarter-pallet: 250 kg max, 551 lbs standard, 2.5 ft height

**Wholesale Bulk:** *Wholesaler > Retailer*

26' Cargo Truck: 8.5 tons max, 10,000 lbs standard, 8-10 ft height

18' Cargo Truck: 3.5 tons max, 4,500 lbs standard, 8 ft height

Pallet Collar: 1,250 lbs max, (8" height, 40" x 48" width)

Cargo-crate: 300 lbs max, 24 gal (20" height, 24" x 24" width)

Milk Crate: 50 lbs max, 4 gal (11" height, 13" x 13" width)

## Facilitation

Native American factories manufacture silicone plastic pallets and crates to reduce operating costs. Lighter materials require less time and resources to move. Their compact designs let us cram more lucrative products per square foot. They last three as long too! Having access to a mass-produced surplus of supplies drops prices below pine! Return plastic transporters and salvaged metal to suppliers to reduce waste.

# Homegrown

## Storage

**Extended Warranty:**

Whenever bud turns stale, run it through a bubble washer. The amount of finger hash accumulated afterwards is too miniscule to do anything else besides toss it into the machine. Molding bricks up to 1 lb. with a pollen press maximizes overall shelf life.

**Love in Every Bite:**

Those who've produced too much rosin will face the dilemma of preventing it from expiring. To rectify this problem, convert excess stockpiles into cannabutter. Then, cook whatever meals your heart desires. Freeze everything you can't eat in a week.

## Dry Goods

**Food Bags:** Flower/Hash

Gallon: "Doggie." Packs storing elbows, half-packs and Q-Ps.

Quart: "Sandwich." Sacks stashing doubles, lids and half-zips.

Pint: "Snack." Bags holding fourths, eights and half-eighths.

Gram: "Sample." Singles pocketing grams and half-grams.

## Fluid Weight

**Spice Jars:** Honey Oil

Quart: (32 fl. oz.). A plastic quart jar = two pints of concentrate.

Pint: (16 fl. oz.) Standard beer cans are 12 oz.; tallboys run 24.

Cup: (8 fl. oz.) Measuring cups are smaller than drinking glasses.

Half-cup: (4 fl. oz.) "Gill." Teacup for hot tea, not iced versions.

Quarter-cup.: (2 oz.) "Jigger." Mixes 1.5 - 1.75 fl. oz. of liquor.

Ounce: (1 fl. oz.). "Shot." Smallest shot size, less than a single.

Tablespoon: (1/2 fl. oz.) One tablespoon = three teaspoons.

Half-table: (1/4$^{th}$ fl. oz.) Half-tablespoon = two drams.

Dram: (1/8$^{th}$ fl. oz.) One dram = 60 drops.

# Review

## Lip Service

**Pulling Strings:**

Product should be no older than the dates I've provided. Otherwise, you'll need to discount your inventory to maintain quotas. Larger CBD farms set aside sugar leaves as an alternative to tobacco paper or leaves for cigar wraps. Edibles are frozen and shipped in Styrofoam boxes containing dry ice to prevent melting or spoilage. Categorize butter by the type of crystalline used, not species or strain. Keep it simple!

Edibles: Refrigerated (2-4 weeks) > Frozen (3-6 months) > Thawed (1-2 weeks)

Hydro: Wholesaler (1-2 months) > Retailer (3-6 months) > Consumer (6-12 months)

Oil: Wholesaler (1-2 months) > Retailer (3-6 months) > Consumer (6-12 months)

Isolate: Wholesaler ($\leq$ 6 months) > Retailer (6-12 months) > Consumer (1-2 years)

Kif: Wholesaler (1-2 years) > Retailer (2-5 years) > Consumer (5-12 years)

Hash: Wholesaler (1-2 years) > Retailer (2-5 years) > Consumer (5-12 years)

## Payments

**Direct Wholesaling:**

Many farmers, factory workers, wholesalers and retailers cover payroll with business checks. Those opting for direct deposit will receive an electronic pay stub for their protection. Acquisition of capital assets, namely vehicles and land, demand cashier's checks. VIP customers can order bulk purchases through apps on their smartphones.

**Behind the Front:**

Dispensaries cannot refuse legal tender from customers, especially when it comes to paying off existing debts. However, they do wish to reduce dependency on hard currency due to theft. Performing cash drops on registers exceeding $500 ensures greater safety during shifts. Wi-Fi card swipers accept sliding, chip and touch screen payments. Medical patients who cannot afford prescriptions can have medication "fronted" to them on a running tab. Credit lines incur low levels of simple interest.

# CHAPTER SEVEN

## *Organic Hydroponics*

### Quadrant 3:1

*Listed below is this chapter's section directory. Topics are grouped together in subsections labeled by underlined bullets. Any further subdivision of information is organized into verses marked by bolded bullets.*

*Overview* ............................................................................. 52

*Artisanal Flower* ................................................................. 53

*Milled Flower* ..................................................................... 55

*Review* ................................................................................ 56

# Overview

## Medical

**Prescriptions:**

Changes in law and industry regulations encourage health insurance companies to cover medical marijuana prescriptions. However, local pharmacies lack the expertise and space dispensaries offer. Patients living too far away from stores place orders on company websites. Whether it's just a gram or several pounds, patients always have access to medication. Anything exceeding what's covered by insurance is full-price.

## Recreational

**Emporium Flagships:**

These hubs combine the roles of recreational dispensary and head shop together. They offer everything from vaping products, specialty tobacco and herbal detoxing. Competition between rival smoke shops is present in every local incorporation, even small towns. Online orders are shipped directly to their customers' their addresses.

**Microdispensaries:**

Microbusinesses can perform deliveries to clients in rural areas and meet them upon request. Unlike larger businesses, they often focus more on their proprietary lines of homegrown goods. Vertical integration ensures freshness and reduced overhead keeps prices down. Mastering the art of producing hash, honey oil, vaporizers, food recipes and paraphernalia could give them a serious edge over potential competitors.

**Dishonest Scales:**

To prevent skimping from dishonest budtenders, all employees must obey two, universal policies: First, only scoop from serving jars underneath displays. Second, zero scales in front of customers. Larger purchases can only be weighed by placing product inside containers. Tare those scales before filling them with product. I've witnessed someone cheat me by purposely calibrating one incorrectly before my own eyes. So, bring a digital scale with you! Report dishonest employees to management.

# Artisanal Flower

## Moonrocks

*(AAAAA, Hand-trimmed, Snowballs)*

Pound: "Elbow." 448 grams is two half-pounds = $3,200.00

Half-pound: "Half-pack." 224 grams is two quarter-pounds = $2,000.00

Quarter-pound: "Q-P." 112 grams is two twin-ounces = 1,200.00

Two-ounce: "Double." 56 grams is ounces = $600.00

Ounce: "Lid." 28 grams is two half-ounces = $350.00

Half-ounce: "Half-zip." 14 grams is two fourths = $240.00

Fourth: "Quad." 7 grams is two eighths = $120.00

Eighth: "Slice." 3.5 grams is two half-eighths = $60.00

Half-eighth: "Teenth" 1.75 grams is one blunt = $30.00

Gram: "Single." One gram is one cigarillo = $20.00

## Private Reserve

*(AAAA, Hand-trimmed, SCROG)*

Cola tops from SCROG grows can produce the fattest, densest, stickiest and frostiest buds known to man! Proper feeding and flushing generates lighter-colored weed.

Pound: "Elbow." 448 grams is two half-pounds = $2,400.00

Half-pound: "Half-pack." 224 grams is two quarter-pounds = $1,500.00

Quarter-pound: "Q-P." 112 grams is two twin-ounces = $900.00

Two-ounce: "Double." 56 grams is ounces = $450.00

Ounce: "Lid." 28 grams is two half-ounces = $270.00

Half-ounce: "Half-zip." 14 grams is two fourths = $180.00

Fourth: "Quad." 7 grams is two eighths = $90.00

Eighth: "Slice." 3.5 grams is two half-eighths = $45.00

Half-eighth: "Teenth" 1.75 grams is one blunt = $25.00

Gram: "Single." One gram is one cigarillo = $15.00

## Premium

*(AAA, Hand-trimmed, SOG)*

Medium-sized nugs set the industry standard for what is to be called a respectable indoor grow. It's not impossible for a master grower to cultivate trips from weed grown in potting mix/soil. Dro appears darker, fluffier and less crystalized than quads.

Pound: "Elbow." 448 grams is two half-pounds = $1,600.00

Half-pound: "Half-pack." 224 grams is two quarter-pounds = $1,000.00

Quarter-pound: "Q-P." 112 grams is two twin-ounces = $600.00

Two-ounce: "Double." 56 grams is ounces = $300.00

Ounce: "Lid." 28 grams is two half-ounces = $180.00

Half-ounce: "Half-zip." 14 grams is two fourths = $120.00

Fourth: "Quad." 7 grams is two eighths = $60.00

Eighth: "Slice." 3.5 grams is two half-eighths = $30.00

Half-eighth: "Teenth" 1.75 grams is one blunt = $15.00

Gram: "Single." One gram is one cigarillo = $10.00

## Smalls

*(AA+, Finger-chopped, Indo)*

To complete customers' orders, budtenders must break nugs into smaller pieces to achieve the correct weights on scales. Doing so creates broken bits called smalls. Smaller colas from stunted plants and popcorn nuggets often fall into this category. Anything finer is designated shake and kept separate for milling pre-ground mixes.

Pound: "Elbow." 448 grams is two half-pounds = $800.00

Half-pound: "Half-pack." 224 grams is two quarter-pounds = $500.00

Quarter-pound: "Q-P." 112 grams is two twin-ounces = $300.00

Two-ounce: "Double." 56 grams is ounces = $150.00

Ounce: "Lid." 28 grams is two half-ounces = $90.00

Half-ounce: "Half-zip." 14 grams is two fourths = $60.00

Fourth: "Quad." 7 grams is two eighths = $30.00

Eighth: "Slice." 3.5 grams is two half-eighths = $15.00

Half-eighth: "Teenth" 1.75 grams is one blunt = $8.00

Gram: "Single." One gram is one cigarillo = $5.00

# Milled Flower

## Shake Mix

*(AA-, Coarse-ground, Indo)*

Shake milled out of organic hydro devoid of sugar leaves is going to be more valuable than stale trim collected off outdoor-grown mids. Prices are comparable to regular.

Pound: "Elbow." 448 grams is two half-pounds = $400.00

Half-pound: "Half-pack." 224 grams is two quarter-pounds = $270.00

Quarter-pound: "Q-P." 112 grams is two twin-ounces = $180.00

Two-ounce: "Double." 56 grams is ounces = $90.00

Ounce: "Lid." 28 grams is two half-ounces = $60.00

Half-ounce: "Half-zip." 14 grams is two fourths = $40.00

Fourth: "Quad." 7 grams is two eighths = $20.00

Eighth: "Slice." 3.5 grams is two half-eighths = $10.00

Half-eighth: "Teenth" 1.75 grams is one blunt = $5.00

## CBD Flower

*(A, Coarse-ground, Indo)*

Hemp is a healthier alternative to tobacco in roll-your-own (RYO) cigarettes, cigarillos and cigars. Honestly, smoking CBD flower in a pipe after getting high is going to be the future. It can also be loaded in tea infusers or used for aromatherapy. Pre-ground product is machine-trimmed by farmers making it more affordable to the public.

Pound: "Elbow." 448 grams is two half-pounds = $200.00

Half-pound: "Half-pack." 224 grams is two quarter-pounds = $135.00

Quarter-pound: "Q-P." 112 grams is two twin-ounces = $90.00

Two-ounce: "Double." 56 grams is ounces = $45.00

Ounce: "Lid." 28 grams is two half-ounces = $30.00

Half-ounce: "Half-zip." 14 grams is two fourths = $20.00

Fourth: "Quad." 7 grams is two eighths = $10.00

Eighth: "Slice." 3.5 grams is two half-eighths = $5.00

# Review

## Hydro

### Diluting the Brand:

Most smoke shops don't manufacture the cannagars and pre-rolls they distribute. Prices aren't determined solely by grammage. Instead, customers pay for branding. Premium cigars containing kif, hashish, rosin, wax or diamonds are more expensive.

### Short Sales:

Flower continues curing during its journey through the supply chain before it reaches consumers. Moreover, some patrons are lighter smokers who might buy in bulk for an entire season. I want the last nugget in their sack to be perfect, not stale! The way to achieve this is by running sales and drop prices further until turnover is achieved.

### Turnover Periods:

Begin discounting bud after three months, two weeks if it's in displays since they oxidize faster due to light and handling. Anything beyond six months partakes in a buy one, get one free deal. If all else fails, give it to your best employees as a bonus.

## Herbs

### Herbal Apothecary:

Kratom boosts energy levels, but in higher doses blocks opioid withdrawals. Wild lettuce treats UTIs, asthma and menstrual cramps. Passion flower alleviates GI problems and insomnia. Ginseng reduces chronic fatigue. Velvet bean replenishes dopamine. Ginger quells nausea and vomiting. Reishi mushrooms elevate mood for those suffering from depression. Kava root clears one's mind while relaxing muscles.

### Detoxification:

Detox bottles are a must in all stores. They're great for drug tests, removing toxins and feeling refreshed. It's important to consume the entire bottle and drink enough water afterwards for them to work properly. Drug tests won't detect them either.

# CHAPTER EIGHT

## *Handcrafted Hashish*

### Quadrant 3:2

Listed below is this chapter's section directory. Topics are grouped together in subsections labeled by underlined bullets. Any further subdivision of information is organized into verses marked by bolded bullets.

*Overview* .................................................................................. 58

*Artisanal Hash* ........................................................................ 59

*Edible Hash* ............................................................................. 62

*Isolate Powder* ....................................................................... 63

*Review* ...................................................................................... 64

# Overview

## Trivia

**Crystalline:**

Homonyms are words with more than one definition. Chemists define crystalline as anything with a crystal-like structure while the cannabis industry uses it to describe THCA isolate. Diamonds geared towards dabbing have much larger crystals. Another distinguishing attribute is the presence of terp sauce, something one can opt out of.

**Bubble Hash:**

Uncles Farm invented Piatella. Pink Champagne is the name of a strain used to make quality, 6-star bubble hash. Moonrocks were invented by Dr. Zodiac and Kurupt. Their trademarks allowed other companies to name entire production styles after them.

## Triad

**Live Rosin:**

Technically, bubble hash made from flash-frozen material contains live terpenes. Yet, pressing it can cause dabs to have the consistency of mashed potatoes. This can be avoided through freeze-drying. Moreover, most of those batches are white because harvesting plants too early gives them immature trichomes. Cold cure blondes (sativa) half a week, browns (balanced) one week and darks (indica) for two weeks.

**Hash Rosin:**

Traditionally, only dry-sifted hashish was used in rosin presses to manufacture hash rosin. However, kif, charas and bubble hash extracted from dried flower are also acceptable. Finger hash is optimal for food-grade rosin (2-star). Anything with higher melt ratings is too wasteful, lacks adequate returns and makes edibles overpriced.

**Flower Rosin:**

Dried plant matter for gummies (1-star). Whenever CBD distilleries press their hemp flower for skin care products instead of edibles, they label the concoction raw oil.

# Artisanal Hash

## Piatella

*(Six-star, Full-melt, Hand-pressed)*

Private reserve hashish. Flash-frozen, top-shelf material is bubble hashed and freeze dried. Cold cure blondes four weeks, browns six and darks eight at drug laboratories.

Pound: "Elbow." 448 grams is two half-pounds = $4,800.00

Half-pound: "Half-pack." 224 grams is two quarter-pounds = $3,000.00

Quarter-pound: "Q-P." 112 grams is two twin-ounces = $1,800.00

Two-ounce: "Double." 56 grams is ounces = $900.00

Ounce: "Lid." 28 grams is two half-ounces = $540.00

Half-ounce: "Half-zip." 14 grams is two fourths = $360.00

Fourth: "Quad." 7 grams is two eighths = $180.00

Eighth: "Slice." 3.5 grams is two half-eighths = $90.00

Half-eighth: "Teenth" 1.75 grams is one blunt = $50.00

Gram: "Single." One gram is one cigarillo = $30.00

## Champagne

*(Six-star, Full-melt, Soft-pressed)*

Pound: "Elbow." 448 grams is two half-pounds = $4,000.00

Half-pound: "Half-pack." 224 grams is two quarter-pounds = $2,400.00

Quarter-pound: "Q-P." 112 grams is two twin-ounces = $1,600.00

Two-ounce: "Double." 56 grams is ounces = $800.00

Ounce: "Lid." 28 grams is two half-ounces = $450.00

Half-ounce: "Half-zip." 14 grams is two fourths = $300.00

Fourth: "Quad." 7 grams is two eighths = $150.00

Eighth: "Slice." 3.5 grams is two half-eighths = $75.00

Half-eighth: "Teenth" 1.75 grams is one blunt = $40.00

Gram: "Single." One gram is one cigarillo = $25.00

## Static Hash

*(Five-star, Full-melt, Hard-pressed)*

Premium hashish. Traditional landraces are slow-dried and dry-cured prior to dry-sieving. Static tech vastly improves dry-sifting. Kif is full-melt (5-star) and buried to age for at least two months. Seal colors: Red (blonde), silver (brown) and gold (dark).

Pound: "Elbow." 448 grams is two half-pounds = $3,200.00

Half-pound: "Half-pack." 224 grams is two quarter-pounds = $2,000.00

Quarter-pound: "Q-P." 112 grams is two twin-ounces = 1,200.00

Two-ounce: "Double." 56 grams is ounces = $600.00

Ounce: "Lid." 28 grams is two half-ounces = $350.00

Half-ounce: "Half-zip." 14 grams is two fourths = $240.00

Fourth: "Quad." 7 grams is two eighths = $120.00

Eighth: "Slice." 3.5 grams is two half-eighths = $60.00

Half-eighth: "Teenth" 1.75 grams is one blunt = $30.00

Gram: "Single." One gram is one cigarillo = $20.00

## Charas

*(Four-star, Half-melt, Hand-rolled)*

Nectar is rubbed off living landrace plants, slow-dried and left to age up to a year. Fingers are hand-rolled to weigh exactly one gram. Machines further hone and polish each ball for eight hours. Performing this by hand in a developed country would've compounded labor cost. Seal colors: Red (blonde), silver (brown) and gold (dark).

Pound: "Elbow." 448 grams is two half-pounds = $2,400.00

Half-pound: "Half-pack." 224 grams is two quarter-pounds = $1,500.00

Quarter-pound: "Q-P." 112 grams is two twin-ounces = $900.00

Two-ounce: "Double." 56 grams is ounces = $450.00

Ounce: "Lid." 28 grams is two half-ounces = $270.00

Half-ounce: "Half-zip." 14 grams is two fourths = $180.00

Fourth: "Quad." 7 grams is two eighths = $90.00

Eighth: "Slice." 3.5 grams is two half-eighths = $45.00

Half-eighth: "Teenth" 1.75 grams is one blunt = $25.00

Gram: "Single." One gram is one cigarillo = $15.00

## Kif (THC)

*(Three-star, Half-melt, Static-sift)*

Dispensary-grade kif. Landrace flower is slow-dried and dry-cured before dry-sieving. Static tech improves dry-sifting. Kif is half-melt (3-star) and buried to age for at least two months. Purer grades of kif are reserved for rolling charas or pressing hashish. Trichome color is based on harvest time: Blonde (early), tan (ripe) and brown (late).

Pound: "Elbow." 448 grams is two half-pounds = $1,600.00

Half-pound: "Half-pack." 224 grams is two quarter-pounds = $1,000.00

Quarter-pound: "Q-P." 112 grams is two twin-ounces = $600.00

Two-ounce: "Double." 56 grams is ounces = $300.00

Ounce: "Lid." 28 grams is two half-ounces = $180.00

Half-ounce: "Half-zip." 14 grams is two fourths = $120.00

Fourth: "Quad." 7 grams is two eighths = $60.00

Eighth: "Slice." 3.5 grams is two half-eighths = $30.00

Half-eighth: "Teenth" 1.75 grams is one blunt = $15.00

Gram: "Single." One gram is one cigarillo = $10.00

## Kif (CBD)

*(Three-star, Half-melt, Static-sift)*

Dispensary-grade kif. CBD-rich hemp is a legal alternative to the Delta-9 found in marijuana. Options: CBD boosts energy, CBG increases creativity and CBN improves sleep habits. THCA and Delta-8 versions were included in the previous price table.

Pound: "Elbow." 448 grams is two half-pounds = $800.00

Half-pound: "Half-pack." 224 grams is two quarter-pounds = $500.00

Quarter-pound: "Q-P." 112 grams is two twin-ounces = $300.00

Two-ounce: "Double." 56 grams is ounces = $150.00

Ounce: "Lid." 28 grams is two half-ounces = $90.00

Half-ounce: "Half-zip." 14 grams is two fourths = $60.00

Fourth: "Quad." 7 grams is two eighths = $30.00

Eighth: "Slice." 3.5 grams is two half-eighths = $15.00

Half-eighth: "Teenth" 1.75 grams is one blunt = $8.00

Gram: "Single." One gram is one cigarillo = $5.00

# Edible Hash

## Edibles

**Baked Goods:**

Most smoke shops don't manufacture the baked edibles they distribute. Prices aren't determined solely by grammage. Instead, customers pay for the brand. Thus, no prices will be listed. UFO cookies (not the strain) contain THCP, special brownies THCH and space cake THCB. I've coined the term UFO cookies to describe an edible rich in THCP.

**Cannabutter:**

All isolate powder is 6-star and full-melt. Private reserve cannabutter relies on cold-cured live rosin instead of hash rosin, both rated as food-grade (2-star), full-spectrum hash. HHC versions are sourced from CBD-rich hemp containing less than 0.3% THC.

THCP Isolate: $480.00 Pound, $240.00 Half-pound, $120.00 Quarter-pound

THCH Isolate: $240.00 Pound, $120.00 Half-pound, $60.00 Quarter-pound

THCB Isolate: $120.00 Pound, $60.00 Half-pound, $30.00 Quarter-pound

Live Rosin: $80.00 Pound, $40.00 Half-pound, $20.00 Quarter-pound

Hash Rosin: $60.00 Pound, $30.00 Half-pound, $15.00 Quarter-pound

## Gummies (THC)

Private reserves capitalize on live rosin (2-star) while the rest utilize flower rosin (1-star). Both types of concentrates are considered food-grade, full-spectrum products.

Live Rosin: (15ct, 1.5 g.) $25.00, (30ct, 3 g.) $50.00, (60ct, 6 g.) $100.00

Delta-9: (15ct, 1.5 g.) $20.00, (30ct, 3 g.) $40.00, (60ct, 6 g.) $80.00

Delta-8: (15ct, 750 mg.) $10.00, (30ct, 1.5 g.) $20.00, (60ct, 3 g.) $40.00

THCV: (15ct, 375 mg.) $5.00, (30ct, 750 mg.) $10.00, (60ct, 3 g.) $20.00

## Gummies (CBD)

CBD: (15ct, 1.5 g.) $5.00, (30ct, 3 g.) $10.00, (60ct., 6 g.) $20.00

CBG: (15ct, 750 mg.) $5.00, (30ct, 1.5 g.) $10.00, (60ct., 3 g.) $20.00

CBN: (15ct, 375 mg.) $5.00, (30ct, 750 mg.) $10.00, (60ct., 1.5 g.) $20.00

# Isolate Powder

## Crystalline

*(Six-star, Full-melt, Decarb)*

THCA is sourced from CBD-rich hemp plants. Delta-9 content is below 0.3%. Heat is required to decarboxylate (decarb) powder if used in edibles, vaporizers, pipes, etc.

Pound: "Elbow." 448 grams is two half-pounds = $6,400.00

Half-pound: "Half-pack." 224 grams is two quarter-pounds = $4,000.00

Quarter-pound: "Q-P." 112 grams is two twin-ounces = 2,400.00

Two-ounce: "Double." 56 grams is ounces = $1,200.00

Ounce: "Lid." 28 grams is two half-ounces = $700.00

Half-ounce: "Half-zip." 14 grams is two fourths = $480.00

Fourth: "Quad." 7 grams is two eighths = $240.00

Eighth: "Slice." 3.5 grams is two half-eighths = $120.00

Half-eighth: "Teenth" 1.75 grams is one blunt = $60.00

Gram: "Single." One gram is one cigarillo = $40.00

## CBD/CBG/CBN

*(Six-star, Full-melt, Decarb)*

Pound: "Elbow." 448 grams is two half-pounds = $5,000.00

Half-pound: "Half-pack." 224 grams is two quarter-pounds = $3,400.00

Quarter-pound: "Q-P." 112 grams is two twin-ounces = $2,000.00

Two-ounce: "Double." 56 grams is ounces = $1,000.00

Ounce: "Lid." 28 grams is two half-ounces = $600.00

Half-ounce: "Half-zip." 14 grams is two fourths = $440.00

Fourth: "Quad." 7 grams is two eighths = $220.00

Eighth: "Slice." 3.5 grams is two half-eighths = $110.00

Half-eighth: "Teenth" 1.75 grams is one blunt = $55.00

Gram: "Single." One gram is one cigarillo = $35.00

# Review

## Marketing

**Inventory Turnover:**

Begin discounting kif, hashish and charas after five years. Offer buy-one, get-one free deals on 12-year-old inventory. Piatella and edibles are refrigerated, cannabutter frozen, to extend their shelf life. Run sales at three months and freebies six months. Isolate powder waits six months before being pushed and one year prior to donation.

**Challenging Charas:**

Fingers beyond two years in age are re-rolled into tosh balls, each weighing one tola (10 g). Once those exceed five years, re-roll them into temple balls (2 oz). Entrust store managers with this task, something they can do while conversating with others. Machines make life easier. Imagine someone banging a tiny gong upon completion!

## Masters

**Frenchy Cannoli:**

Didier Camilleri was a renowned master hashishin responsible for setting industry standards on bubble hash. He was famous for his temple balls, some aged up to 12 years. Being born in France prior to moving to California gave rise to his nickname.

**Club des Hashischins:**

Headquartered at Hôtel de Lauzun in Paris during 1844-1849 A.D. This research group experimented with edible hash. Afterwards, the organization disbanded. Cannabis wasn't harming them, but was deemed unnecessary by those following their dreams.

**Order of Assassins:**

Founded by Hasan al-Sabbah, this Nizari Ismaili sect inspired the word assassination. Hashish is a corruption of their name, Hashshashin, which is Arabic for "hashish smoker." They were accused by Egyptians as hashish-eaters. Subsequently, those found guilty in that country of doing so had their teeth pulled and crops burned.

# CHAPTER NINE

## *Honey Oil Concentrates*

### Quadrant 3:3

*Listed below is this chapter's section directory. Topics are grouped together in subsections labeled by underlined bullets. Any further subdivision of information is organized into verses marked by bolded bullets.*

*Overview* ........................................................................... 66

*Cold-start Dabbing* ........................................................... 67

*Atomized Vaping* .............................................................. 69

*Homemade Oil* .................................................................. 70

*Review* .............................................................................. 74

# Overview

## Display

**Presentation:**

Vaporizer sections elevate pod devices as top-shelf, mods mid-grade and disposables bottom-shelf items. Judge dabs according to their extraction methods. $CO_2$ is top-tier, ethanol premium goods and petrochemicals affordable, old-school throwbacks. Display cases should be chilled and restocked by refrigerators located in store rooms.

**Turnover Periods:**

Factories cold-cure hash oil up to two weeks before releasing warehouse shipments. Product ages no more than 1-2 months by the time wholesalers supply retail chains. Begin discounting inventory after three months, two weeks if it's in displays since they oxidize faster due to light and handling. Anything beyond six months partakes in a buy one, get one free deal. If that fails, give it to your best employees as a bonus. Doing so ensures all concentrate is consumed within its 12-month expiration date.

## Detection

**Counterfeit Wax:**

Fake shatter contains pine resin, something that congeals in the lungs of dabbers. Doing so can kill customers! There are two ways to test wax: Heat and alcohol. Staff place a dab on a metal spoon, apply heat via flame, rub their finger in it, wait several seconds and peel it off. Pure wax will smear while counterfeits slough off easily. Customers drop a dab into warm isopropyl alcohol (91%). Authentic merch quickly dissolves whenever stirred; the imposter releases white residue and becomes syrupy.

**Oil Degradation:**

Expiring extracts exhibit a change in four attributes: Color, consistency, smoothness and flavor. Darkening over time is the maturation of CBN, but reddening indicates spoilage via oxidation. Crust pockets form in containers and wax loses its appealing texture. Vapor feels harsh in one's throat and lungs. Flavor and aroma diminish too.

# Cold-start Dabbing

## **Live Sugar**

Private reserve hash oil. $CO_2$ diamonds with fine grains resembling isolate powder smothered in terp sauce. Proper freeze-drying and cold curing impacts overall flavor.

Pound: "Elbow." 448 grams is two half-pounds = $6,400.00

Half-pound: "Half-pack." 224 grams is two quarter-pounds = $4,000.00

Quarter-pound: "Q-P." 112 grams is two twin-ounces = 2,400.00

Two-ounce: "Double." 56 grams is ounces = $1,200.00

Ounce: "Lid." 28 grams is two half-ounces = $700.00

Half-ounce: "Half-zip." 14 grams is two fourths = $480.00

Fourth: "Quad." 7 grams is two eighths = $240.00

Eighth: "Slice." 3.5 grams is two half-eighths = $120.00

Half-eighth: "Teenth" 1.75 grams is two singles = $60.00

Gram: "Single." One gram is 24 dabs = $40.00

Half-gram: "Half-g." One half-gram is 12 dabs = $20.00

## **Sugar Wax**

Pound: "Elbow." 448 grams is two half-pounds = $5,000.00

Half-pound: "Half-pack." 224 grams is two quarter-pounds = $3,400.00

Quarter-pound: "Q-P." 112 grams is two twin-ounces = $2,000.00

Two-ounce: "Double." 56 grams is ounces = $1,000.00

Ounce: "Lid." 28 grams is two half-ounces = $600.00

Half-ounce: "Half-zip." 14 grams is two fourths = $440.00

Fourth: "Quad." 7 grams is two eighths = $220.00

Eighth: "Slice." 3.5 grams is two half-eighths = $110.00

Half-eighth: "Teenth" 1.75 grams is two singles = $55.00

Gram: "Single." One gram is 24 dabs = $35.00

Half-gram: "Half-g." One half-gram is 12 dabs = $17.50

## Live Nectar

Premium resin. Refining this $CO_2$ extract further creates two other goods: Terp sauce and sugar diamonds! Redirect excess caches towards the manufacturing of these two concentrates. Nectar and live sauce resemble rosin diamonds drenched in terp sauce. The proper name of this wonderful, flavorful liquid is high terpene extract, or HTE.

Pound: "Elbow." 448 grams is two half-pounds = $4,800.00

Half-pound: "Half-pack." 224 grams is two quarter-pounds = $3,000.00

Quarter-pound: "Q-P." 112 grams is two twin-ounces = $1,800.00

Two-ounce: "Double." 56 grams is ounces = $900.00

Ounce: "Lid." 28 grams is two half-ounces = $360.00

Half-ounce: "Half-zip." 14 grams is two fourths = $180.00

Fourth: "Quad." 7 grams is two eighths = $180.00

Eighth: "Slice." 3.5 grams is two half-eighths = $90.00

Half-eighth: "Teenth" 1.75 grams is two singles = $50.00

Gram: "Single." One gram is 24 dabs = $30.00

Half-gram: "Half-g." One half-gram is 12 dabs = $15.00

## Live Sap

Premium rosin. Separating lipids from oils results in the formation of $CO_2$ resin and wax. Commit excess caches towards manufacturing these two concentrates. Proper live sap and live rosin should retain a fiery, golden tinge with creamier nucleation.

Pound: "Elbow." 448 grams is two half-pounds = $4,000.00

Half-pound: "Half-pack." 224 grams is two quarter-pounds = $2,400.00

Quarter-pound: "Q-P." 112 grams is two twin-ounces = $1,600.00

Two-ounce: "Double." 56 grams is ounces = $800.00

Ounce: "Lid." 28 grams is two half-ounces = $450.00

Half-ounce: "Half-zip." 14 grams is two fourths = $300.00

Fourth: "Quad." 7 grams is two eighths = $150.00

Eighth: "Slice." 3.5 grams is two half-eighths = $75.00

Half-eighth: "Teenth" 1.75 grams is two singles = $40.00

Gram: "Single." One gram is 24 dabs = $25.00

Half-gram: "Half-g." One half-gram is 12 dabs = $12.50

# Atomized Vaping

## Full-spectrum

**Dabbing Cartridges:**

Mods house refillable tanks while pods employ disposable cartridges. Both options offer the same quality honey oil presents to dabbers. In fact, dab pens let their users load dabs directly into them! Few realize that the act of dabbing itself is technically a primitive form of vaping oil. Companies marketing specialty items, those with tanks exceeding 3-10 grams, should influence their pricing in accordance to the list below.

Live Sugar: $20.00 half-gram, $40 gram, $80.00 twin-gram

Sugar Wax: $17.50 half-gram, $35 gram, $70.00 twin-gram

Live Nectar: $15.00 half-gram, $30.00 gram, $60.00 twin-gram

Live Sap: $12.50 half-gram, $25.00 gram, $50.00 twin-gram

**$CO_2$ Disposables:**

As demand shifts towards the four extracts above, their direct predecessors become more affordable. Now, everyone can have affordable, 100% organic, $CO_2$ oil! Rosin diamonds are solventless because they're birthed by punching live rosin in presses.

Rosin Diamonds: $12.50 half-gram, $25 gram, $50.00 twin-gram

Crumble Wax: $10.00 half-gram, $20 gram, $40.00 twin-gram

Live Sauce: $7.50 half-gram, $15.00 gram, $30.00 twin-gram

Live Rosin: $5.00 half-gram, $10.00 gram, $20.00 twin-gram

## Broad-spectrum

**Steam Distillation:**

Raw crude (1-star) and refined essential (2-star) oil are rated as food-grade items. Only distillate should be vaped, let alone dabbed. CBD, CBG and CBN selections are now infused with natural hemp terpenes! Excess terp sauce generated during isolate production is added to distillate. Leave artificial flavoring to the tobacco industry!

Distillate: $5.00 half-gram, $10 gram, $20.00 twin-gram

Essential: $5.00 (7.5 ml), $10.00 (15 ml), $20.00 (30 ml)

Crude: $5.00 (15 ml), $10.00 (30 ml), $20.00 (60 ml)

# Homemade Oil

## Full-extract

**Rick Simpson Oil:**

RSO, aka phoenix tears. Medical patients use isopropyl alcohol to extract crude oil from flower to make their own homemade edibles. This food-grade concentrate is decarboxylated before being injected into empty capsules to administer microdoses.

**Full-extract Cannabis Oil:**

FECO, aka green dragon. Ethanol alcohol is 100% organic, less toxic, more affordable, renewable, consumed regularly in beverages and added to unleaded gasoline! Apart from differences in solvents used, both versions follow the same recipe listed below.

## IHO/EHO

**Supplies List:**

Isopropyl ($\geq$ 91%) or ethanol ($\geq$ 150-proof). Blender, tall mason jar, cheesecloth, short wide-mouth jar, shoelace or string, crock-pot, oscillating fan and slow-dried flower.

**Blending:**

Place alcohol in freezer; you'll need it in an hour. Fill blender $1/3^{rd}$ full to avoid jamming. Coarse-grind material and dump it into your tall mason jar leaving the top $1/5^{th}$ empty. Repeat these steps until all remaining marijuana has been processed.

**Soaking:**

Rinse remaining residue out of blender with alcohol into said jar. Cover milled bud with isopropyl. Stir for 2-5 minutes. Rest jar in freezer 45 minutes to several hours.

**Cooking:**

Lay cheesecloth over wide-mouth jar secured by a shoelace. Squeeze remaining oil out. Fill crock-pot with enough warm water to line up with the solvent. Set it on high in a well-ventilated place to boil, leave the lid open and supervise it for 3-4 hours. Towards the end, check batches every 15 minutes. Viscosity should match molasses.

**Infusion:**

Load syringes to inject microdoses into said capsules. Remember: D9 is 2-3x stronger than D8, itself 2-3x more than THCV! Additionally, you can't corner or halve them like you do gummies. So, beginners take 5 mg, regulars 10 mg and experts 20 mg doses.

# Resin

### Snap n' Pull:

Taffy's attributes are an appearance resembling brittle and malleability consistent to chewing gum. An abundance in terpenes gives it greater moisture than wax. Butane imparts reddish-brown coloration. Taffy rosin is a pale, novelty version of live rosin.

### Live Resin:

Ethanol varieties retain their deep amber hue and heavy viscosity. Only flash-frozen flower is used. Low-grade oil is oftentimes runny, straw-colored and bland. Similar to Piatella, the words live sauce and live nectar also began as their companies' brands.

# BHO

### Supplies List:

Butane canister, blender, extraction tube, cheesecloth, hose clamp, glass bowl, crock-pot, Pyrex dish, oscillating fan and dried flower. Some hose clamps need drum keys, others flathead screwdrivers. Always leave windows open or operate outdoors!

### Blending:

Freeze solvent until it's -13°F. Fill blender 1/3$^{rd}$ full to avoid jamming. Coarse-grind material and dump it in your extraction tube. Cover end with cheesecloth secured by a hose clamp. Dispense solvent for 3 ½ minutes. Wearing gloves protects skin from freezer burn or gangrene. Blow into tube to clear out any remaining hydrocarbons.

### Purging:

Fill crock-pot with enough warm water to line up with the solvent and set it on low. Once a temperature of 70-85°F has been achieved, leave lid open and supervise resin for 1-2 hours. Check batches every 15 minutes. Viscosity should match chewing gum.

# EHO

### Supplies List:

Ethanol (200-proof). Blender, tall mason jar, cheesecloth, short wide-mouth jar, shoelace, crock-pot, Pyrex oven tray, oscillating fan and flash-frozen flower. Execute FECO recipe and ready this full-extract concentrate before performing the next step.

### Modifications:

Lay cheesecloth over wide-mouth jar secured by a shoelace. Squeeze remaining oil out. Fill crock-pot with enough warm water to line up with solvent. Set on medium in a well-ventilated place to simmer, leave lid open and supervise 3-4 hours. Towards finale, check every 15 minutes. Viscosity should match syrup before cold-curing.

## Wax

### BudderKing's Butter:

A Canadian man nicknamed BudderKing invented budder. Knock-offs drove him to trademark his butter, but he was forced to purposely misspell it. Propane hash oil is fairer in color, creamier in consistency, way tastier and smoother to smoke than BHO.

### Live Badder:

Batter differs for three reasons: Only flash-frozen plant material can be used, hence the presence of live terpenes. There's more whipping involving and longer time spent purging solvents. Ethanol gives batter a new lease on life and even creamier texture.

## PHO

### Supplies List:

Propane canister, blender, extraction tube, cheesecloth, hose clamp, glass bowl, crockpot, Pyrex dish, oscillating fan and dried flower. Some hose clamps need drum keys, others flathead screwdrivers. Always leave windows open or operate outdoors!

### Blending:

Freeze solvent until it's -13°F. Fill blender 1/3$^{rd}$ full to avoid jamming. Coarse-grind material and dump it in your extraction tube. Cover end with cheesecloth secured by a hose clamp. Dispense solvent for 3 ½ minutes. Wearing gloves protects skin from freezer burn or gangrene. Blow into tube to clear out any remaining hydrocarbons.

### Purging:

Fill crock-pot with enough warm water to line up with the solvent. Set it on high to boil, leave lid open and supervise for 1-2 hours. Larger runs could take a half-day, sometimes an entire day! Lay batches in Pyrex dishes and bake them in a 250°F oven for 30-45 minutes. Stir wax until oil resembles restaurant-grade compound butter.

## EHO

### Supplies List:

Ethanol ($\geq$ 180-proof). Blender, tall mason jar, cheesecloth, short wide-mouth jar, shoelace, crock-pot, Pyrex oven tray, oscillating fan and flash-frozen flower. Execute FECO recipe and ready this full-extract concentrate before performing the next step.

### Modifications:

Lay batches in Pyrex oven tray and bake them in a 250°F oven for 30-45 minutes. Stir wax until EHO resembles whipped cream. Freeze-dry and cold-cure concentrates. Strive to achieve the creamy, moist texture of PHO budder through trial and error.

# Diamonds

**BudderKing's Shatter:**

Brittle predates diamonds and shatters upon impact. Acetone gives batches the best of both worlds. It's cleaner too! Propane makes dabs too wet and extracts less cannabinoids. Butane imparts a darker, unsightly color with blander flavors/aroma.

**Live Diamonds:**

Flash-frozen material yields live terpenes. Substitute hydrocarbons with a centrifuge. Unlike sugar, resin is spun causing large THCA crystals and terp sauce to separate. Decarboxylate and suspend them in live resin to create liquid diamonds. Terp sauce further boosts flavor, aroma and the entourage effect itself enhancing users' highs.

# AHO

**Supplies List:**

Acetone ($\geq$ 99% purity), blender, coffee filters (90-micron), short wide-mouth jar, shoelace or string, Pyrex oven dish, box cutter, oscillating fan and dried flower. Place acetone in the freezer for an hour. Always leave a window open or operate outdoors!

**Blending:**

Fill blender $1/3^{rd}$ full to avoid jamming. Coarse-grind material and dump it in your wide-mouth jar. Rinse blender with acetone, incorporate any remaining residue into the batch and immediately pour solvent over milled flower until fully-covered. Keep the top $1/5^{th}$ of jar empty. Don't shake marinade while it soaks for exactly 3 minutes. Secure two or more filters with shoelace and begin straining liquid into Pyrex tray.

**Purging:**

Bake them in a 250°F oven for 30-45 minutes. Keep the door open. Avoid stirring wax. Finished product should resemble fiery, gold-colored peanut brittle. Cool before smashing portions. Cold-cure portions in your refrigerator. Dab whenever necessary.

# EHO

**Supplies List:**

Ethanol ($\geq$ 190-proof), blender, tall mason jar, cheesecloth, wide-mouth jar, shoelace, crock-pot, Pyrex dish, centrifuge, tube vials, oscillating fan and flash-frozen flower. Execute FECO recipe, ready full-extract and vials' tube linings before moving forward.

**Modifications:**

Load each tube and centrifuge evenly. Run machines for 1-2 hours making sure to replace warm linings every 30 minutes. Cold-cure dabs in refrigerator as needed.

# Review

## Solvents

**CBD-rich Hemp:**

Commercial growers have access to steam distilleries those at home must rely on petrochemical solvents. Acetate, pentane and hexane parallel acetone, propane and butane. Heptane belongs in drug labs churning out hallucinogenic DMT cartridges.

<u>Centrifuge</u>: Separates isolate from terp sauce. Add excess HTE to distillate.

<u>Ethyl Acetate</u>: Optimum solvent geared towards creating purified distillate.

<u>Pentane</u>: Excels at refining essential oil in the absence of proper steam kettles.

<u>Hexane</u>: Extracts raw crude oil. Solvent is also used to make vegetable oil.

## Sagas

**Phil Salazar:**

Phil "Soil-grown" Salazar invented rosin tech in 2015. While living in Southern California, he accidentally discovered this solventless technology. Whenever Phil couldn't obtain full-melt hash, he'd he use a hair straightener to thin his extracts so they'd dab better. Although Afghanis have made hash rosin in a similar fashion for centuries, this discovery inspired Soil-grown to patent the rosin press design itself!

**Passing the Dab:**

During the '60s, soldiers participating in the Vietnam War readily purchased weed from locals and began using petrol and acetone to fabricate the original dabs. Honey oil has been around for millennia, but was never dabbed until some G.I.s got creative!

**François Rabelais:**

Frenchman who discovered cannabis' flower rosin. France's first great prose writer lived between 1483-1553. Rabelais also doubled as a monk and physician. One of his posthumous literary works included marijuana rosin he dubbed "rosée de Provence." Eventually, this perfumed oil evolved into the flower rosin we see in today's edibles.

# CHAPTER TEN

## *Paraphernalia Items*

### Quadrant 3:4

*Listed below is this chapter's section directory. Topics are grouped together in subsections labeled by underlined bullets. Any further subdivision of information is organized into verses marked by bolded bullets.*

Overview ............................................................................................ 76

Traditional Pipes ............................................................................... 77

Conversion Kits ................................................................................. 78

Modern Vaporizers ........................................................................... 79

Review ................................................................................................ 80

# Overview

## **Size Matters**

**Indian Hookah:**

Abul-Fath Gilani was a Persian physician accredited with inventing the waterpipe: Hookahs and bongs! Hookahs originated in India letting users smoke tobacco, opium and hash through hoses. Metal designs gave way to ceramics, then borosilicate glass.

**Thai Bong:**

Bong is Thai for bamboo pipe and the Hmong people made them famous. Scythian tribes honored royal burials dating back to 400 B.C. with gold pipes. Ethiopians built theirs out of pottery and animal horns. However, none of these ancient relics were ever authentic waterpipes. Therefore, they're gourds, not bongs! Bob Snodgrass is the godfather of the glass movement usurping ceramic's popularity during the '60s.

**American Dab Rig:**

HMK and JP Toro of Toro Glass pioneered dab rigs. Butane torch lighters heat nails prior to loading dabs. Smaller versions were nicknamed dab straws. Most wet vapes we see today were inspired by the concept of dab pens; load honey, then atomize it.

## **Secret Fire**

**Chillum Chalice:**

Indians performed Hindu ceremonies venerating Shiva while smoking chillums. Usage required holding them at an upward angle along with one's hand closing any air gaps between the mouthpiece and their lips. Rastafarian Jamaicans modified these into large waterpipes resembling large African gourds chambered to house bong water.

**Spoon Bubbler:**

Wooden pipes are still used to this day to smoke tobacco, although they're a dying breed. Ceramics eventually gave way to modern glasswork. Contemporary upgrades dubbed bubblers incorporate water filtration to cool fresh smoke before inhalation.

# Traditional Pipes

## Waterpipes

**Traditional Hookahs:**

Optimizes kif, kief mixes and shisha tobacco. Taller and thinner than modern designs. Borosilicate body, round bottom, four rubber hoses, stainless tray and coal basket. To carburate a hookah, simply pull one of the hoses out of its purge valve. Decorate entry-levels with antique bronze, grant mid-grades silver and adorn top-tiers in gold.

**Gravity Hookahs:**

Hash pipe. Stündenglass invented these. Their compact design made them portable and they double as cocktail smokers too! Borosilicate chambers, silicone-based flat-bottom, rubber hose and temperature control buttons. Modules accept concentrate.

**Dab Rigs:**

Authentic full-melt experience! Borosilicate body, flat bottom and angled neck are key features. Recyclers rely on chambers to force smoke to continue purifying itself by re-entering water chambers. Entry-levels get one, mid-grades two and top-tiers three.

**Water Bongs:**

Blazes mids. Borosilicate body, beaker-shaped bottom and straight neck. Percolators purify smoke. Entry-level minis get one, mid-grade standards two and a top-tier talls three. There are too many types of percolators to list, but honeycomb designs always win. Removing the bowl, itself attached to a male downstem, activates carburetors.

## Bubblers

**Water Chillums:**

Charas! Borosilicate body without carbs. Ice water can be added or drained through the mouthpiece or bowl. Entry-level one-hitters are quite small. Mid-grade dugouts conceal a one-hitter, extra cannabis and cleaning tool split across three chambers. Large steamrollers might have carbs and resemble a miniature bong without water.

**Spoon Bubs:**

Conserves dro. Scientific glass (borosilicate) body with carburetor (hole). Users take their thumb off carbs to clear excessive smoke out of chambers. Ice water can be added or drained through the mouthpiece, carb or bowl. Size and girth determines if a pipe is entry-level, mid-grade or top-tier rendering acrylic and ceramic obsolete.

# Conversion Kits

## Adaptors

**Hookah E-bowls:**

Electronic bowls convert hookahs into vaporizers rendering traditional coal trays obsolete. Another added benefit besides reducing carcinogens includes more precise temperature control and vapor output. Again, issue similar batteries and USB cables.

**Rig E-nails:**

Most kits contain three parts. You'll need to create a universal downspout adapter. A rubber stopper can expand and contract to handle different-sized holes. The nail needs a handle so you can pull it out to carburate the bong without burning your fingers. The dome and nail are both quartz. Dabbing kits are described on the review.

**Bong E-bowls:**

Wands are slides transforming water bongs into dry vapes. Smaller versions should be manufactured to fit bubblers and spoon pipes. Similar to our aforementioned e-joints, they're powered by built-in lithium battery systems recharged by USB cables.

**Bubbler E-bowls:**

Converting traditional chillums into vapes is tricky because they require a grooved stone to block debris from being inhaled. Both types of handheld pipes from the previous page pose a design challenge since water must be kept away from electrical components at all times. Different models often have larger bowls than others too.

## Holders

**E-joints:**

Portable, dry herb vaporizer lets users shove everything from spliffs, joints, cigarillos and blunts into said device! As the built-in atomizer burns through their RYO (roll-your-own), the heating element drops along with it. For joints with filters, place butts atop the built-in pin. Include USB charging cables. Butts have filters; roaches don't.

**Reefer Madness:**

Spliffs contain weed and kief kif; both are marijuana cigarettes. Cones are fat, funnel-shaped, doobies and pinners skinny joints. Sweets are small and blunts medium-sized cigars. Their namesake comes from the tobacco paper they're rolled in. If the cigar is wrapped in tobacco leaves, it's a dutch. An authentic cannagar uses cannabis leaves.

# Modern Vaporizers

## Dry Herb

**E-hookah Vapes:**

Miniature desktop hookah! Their ovens combine convection and conduction heating (hybrid). Twisted, stainless steel coils supplant coal baskets. Borosilicate body, round bottom, two rubber hoses and stainless steel loading tray. Session vapes completely consume whatever cannabis is loaded forcing stoners to commit to their decisions.

**Volcano Packs:**

Similar to gravity bongs, these sessions have a balloon serving as a detachable lung containing the vapor users inhale. Anything that's too much for one person to handle should be passed to others before it goes stale. A multi-wrapped, nickel coil powers their convection ovens. Silicone-based flat bottom and temperature control buttons.

**Dry Mods:**

Premium portable. Mesh net coil with triple strands, conduction oven, silicone body and quartz bowl. Features elaborate temperature and volume control buttons for experienced users seeking maximum customization to suit their "on-the-go" needs.

**Dry Pods:**

Simplified portability. User-friendly and less complicated to operate. Dual ceramic coil system, built-in conduction oven, silicone body and quartz bowl. All four dry herb models have horizontal coils while wet oil vapes standardize vertical coil technology.

## Wet Oil

**Box Mods:**

Modified flashlight. Triple-stranded, Kanthal (FeCrAl) coil combines iron, chromium and aluminum. They can endure 3,300 °F! Silicone body houses a refillable reservoir.

**Pod Kits:**

Disposable carts contain a dual nichrome (NiCr) coil comprised of nickel, chromium and iron. Trace amounts of manganese and silicon may also be present. Silicone body.

**Disposables:**

Successor to the dab pen. Titanium coil, silicone body and reservoir tank. Brands may include a switch to mix different oils together isolated in segregated chambers.

# Review

## Nails

**Hot Nails:**

Nails are shaped like the bowls/trays resting atop of hookahs. Quartz nails were superseded by ceramics, but found a new lease on life as bangers. Ultimately, titanium won. Anyone patient enough to properly season them, albeit consume slightly more oil to do so, won't experience a metallic aftertaste. Cleaning techniques prevent oxidation, thus limiting toxicity. Experienced individuals who've mastered the art of heating them can execute low-temp hits or fire up hot dabs all on one nail.

**Bangin' Bangers:**

Buckets are easier to ready and clean afterwards. Terp spinners help disperse flavor and temperature more evenly. Terp slurpers can handle higher volumes without getting overwhelmed. Their design combines the next two things together: Control towers feature a loading tray and tube separated by a quartz pill. Smoke enters charmers through a pearl. Marbles are spherical carb caps monopolized by slurpers. The stem is its neck. Joints connect bangers to dab rigs; some male, others female.

**Carb Caps:**

Inappropriate pairings generate rapid temperature fluctuations between materials, which can eventually, sometimes immediately, crack nails. Always match quartz, ceramic and titanium with itself. Slanted bangers demand slanted, aka universal caps while flat buckets accept bubbles. Some designs include spinners too! Much like the potheads who consume dabs, picks for loading concentrate are also called dabbers.

## Bowls

**Liberty Bowls:**

Quartz funnels' transparency showcases the combustion process. Ceramic standards preserve flavor, but stainless steel slides (bowls with handles) are king. Ash catchers loaded underneath stop debris from being inhaled upon cashing (finishing) pieces.

# CHAPTER ELEVEN
## *Stationary Sessions*

### Quadrant 4:1

*Listed below is this chapter's section directory. Topics are grouped together in subsections labeled by underlined bullets. Any further subdivision of information is organized into verses marked by bolded bullets.*

*Overview* .................................................................................... 82

*Vaping Culture* ........................................................................... 83

*The Waterworks* ........................................................................ 85

*Dabbing Rigs* ............................................................................. 87

*Review* ....................................................................................... 88

# Overview

## **Honored**

**Heroic Microdoses:**

Beginners rapidly develop tolerances comfortably by microdosing gummies from reputable sources. Score stronger edibles in halves, quarters or whatever fraction is deemed necessary. From personal experience, some were potent enough to force me to cut them into 24 pieces! Wait at least 2-4 hours for them to peak before ingesting more. Taking eddies on a full stomach and one's own metabolism affect performance. Once sustaining the habit becomes unaffordable, transition to vaping.

Hero: THCV (100 mg), D8 (50 mg), D9 (20 mg).

Macro: THCV (50 mg), D8 (25 mg), D9 (10 mg).

Micro: THCV (25 mg), D8 (12.5 mg), D9 (5 mg).

## **Handpicked**

**Paying Pied Pipers:**

Bowls prefer fresher bud than blunts or joints, but having a higher moisture content causes grinders to clog with resin. Breaking up nuggets by hand exposes tiny stems hidden deep within them. Herb grinders pulverize them and mix everything together. The wraps used by people who roll up weed mask these off-putting flavors. Ironically, pipes designed to produce the purest smoke make every imperfection noticeable.

**Sliced n' Diced:**

Slice hash over a cutting board with a hot knife. I recommend acquiring at least one butane blowtorch and heating said utensil until red-hot. Bestow coarse chop to pressed hashish, medium dicing towards rolled charas and fine mincing on flower.

Coarse: Hashish (full-melt). Nicknamed finger/rough chop.

Medium: Charas (half-melt). Dicing parallels coarse-grind.

Fine: Flower. Mincing is equivalent to a medium-grind.

# Vaping Culture

## Liquid

**Disposables:**

Economy options catering to on-demand microdosing while limiting waste. Some come pre-charged while others require charging with a micro-USB cable. Avoid tilting them upside down in your pocket. Otherwise, they'll leak! Unclog devices by slicing the end off a cotton swab and inserting it in mouthpieces. Oxidized oil turns dark red.

**Pod Kits:**

Interchangeable cartridges allow users to switch between marijuana, Delta-8, CBD, nicotine and DMT all on one device! Quality carts feature natural terpenes. A blinker challenge involves holding down the button while hitting said device until it blinks.

**Box Mods:**

Think of pods as an alternative to dab straws and mods dab rigs for on-the-go usage. Each person can adjust vapor output accommodating one's own lung capacity. If a group of friends rented a hotel room during a road trip, they could pass this around to their stoner buddies while one of them gets a nicotine fix puffing on a pod cart.

## Herb

**Dry Pods:**

Consider this the spoon pipe of modern vaping! Swapping carts lets users sample several strains at once or conserve dro. Some people enjoy smoking CBD flower instead of hitting cheap pens. There's no need for ashtrays, burn holes or lingering stench in clothing. Passing one around after hotboxing your dry mod is always fun.

**Dry Mods:**

Paralleling bongs, dry mods excel at baking both weed and hash in general. Whenever someone insists on grinding bud instead of chopping it by hand, encourage them to deposit the nuggets' keef accumulating underneath grinders into their host's oven.

**E-joints:**

Joints and blunts presented by guests can be vaped safely by younger, more affluent, health-conscious generations. Turning rolls controls any potential running. Be sure to discard butts if they're present. I don't recommend vaping full-sized, tobacco-filled cigars because most connoisseurs enjoy shoving them in their mouths like snuff.

# Desktop

**E-hookahs:**

Session vapes guarantee smoother toking and unrivaled flavor than their handheld counterparts. Some e-hookahs maintain water filtration. Desktops rest atop tables eliminating the need to hold them meaning no one fears dropping them. Tobacco can be consumed indoors without leaving any lingering odor or staining interior fabric.

**Volcano Packs:**

Dry herb version of the gravity bong. Devices rely on temperature and volume control options instead of water filtration. Lungs are detachable and passed around by their gatherings. While some guests partake in getting inebriated, others can enjoy an e-hookah loaded with tobacco. Doing so keeps volcanos clean reducing maintenance.

# Conversion

**Nameless Mists:**

Japan's 2024 amendments to its drug laws permitted cultivation and prescription usage of medical marijuana. Yet, numerous apartment and condominium projects prohibit smoking on patios and balconies. Working-class residents hang their clothes out to dry outside forcing tenants to smoke in the parking lots. Smaller units make it easier for neighbors down the hallway to take notice and some people are allergic to weed smoke. Moreover, hotboxing in these circumstances could trigger fire alarms.

**Forced Adaptation:**

Modern vapes do a better job conserving cannabis, but waterpipes are fun for special occasions! Conversion kits are the only way these individuals get away with using them. E-bowls convert hand pipes, bongs and hookahs while e-nails target dab rigs.

**Shadow Force:**

Not everyone drives a beat-up work truck they can smoke in! Purchasing new or high-end vehicles, carpooling in one owned by someone who doesn't bestow occupants smoking rights or dating fussy girlfriends hostile towards one's habits is more than enough reason to make the switch towards vaping. Certain professions demand employees who don't reek of tobacco or cannabis at work. However, nicotine patches and gum designed to help addicts quit show up on drug tests. Whoever refuses them employment over this issue is both unreasonable and downright unconstitutional!

**Model Citizens:**

Vaping doesn't stain teeth nearly as fast as smoking does. There's no need to douse oneself in body spray, chew gum or pop breath mints. It's easier on one's heart and lungs too. Dry herb products contain less vitamin E acetate, itself guilty of causing lung injuries leading to fluid buildup, breathlessness, dry coughing and chest pain.

# The Waterworks

## Bubblers

**Spoon Pipes:**

Housing conditions accepting towards smoking can indulge in combusting quality cannabis indoors or rolled goods outdoors. Handhelds are perfect for 1-2 people smoking dro. Purchasing pipes from head shops doesn't demand learning how to construct homemade pipes nor does it accost the virgin lungs of young health nuts. Much like every pipe listed in this section, corner the bowl so everyone gets greens.

**Chillums/Steamrollers:**

Anyone who wants to smoke a blunt or joint outside without holding it in their hand can load fatties in traditional chillums! This life hack prevents fingers from staining with resin, smelling smoky or needing washing to rectify either effect. Steamrollers are dry pipes, yet rolled weed doesn't necessitate water filtration present in bongs.

## Ghettos

**Fruit Pipes:**

Contrary to the others below, these produce items are technically considered bongs. Start with an apple! Yank stem out, gut a pen, shove said item horizontally through apple to create two holes (mouthpiece/carb) and bore core until it reaches tunnel (bowl). Perform test run by blowing into fruit and eat it afterwards. You're welcome!

**Aluminum Foil:**

Repeated folding reinforces strength. Fold flared, top section to create a bowl (some people add a faucet aerator) and crimp mouthpiece. Dispose after finishing session.

**Soft Drink Cans:**

Pop can's top off. Smoke rises, so face opening upward (mouthpiece). Poke holes with a tack on upward-facing side (bowl), crinkle it inward slightly so weed won't fall off and punch a fat hole on one side (carb). FYI: Russia considered beer a soft drink!

**Paper Towel Rolls:**

Cardboard steamroller. Slice a small section off and fashion a tiny funnel (bowl). Drill it into the upward facing side towards the opposing end leaving a few inches (carb). Installing a foil-made bowl is a secondary option. Slides recovered from broken bongs are the final alternative. Prisoners often craft these out of empty, toilet paper rolls.

## Waterpipes

**Water Bongs:**

Medium-sized groups (2-4 people) might load small bowls for each participant called snaps. They gift greens to everyone without having to corner and are intended to be cashed (finished) in one hit. Doing so is taking it to the face. Liberty bowls house an eighth of cannabis. Bongs are commonly associated with friends lounging on sofas.

**Traditional Hookahs:**

Groups guilty of having at least one member who smokes cigarettes need a hookah. Setting them in garages with their garage doors cracked open for ventilation solves every problem encountered while consuming pipe tobacco. Molasses gives shisha its pleasant aroma and isn't recommended for use in other pipes, even gravity hookahs.

**Gravity Hookahs:**

Modifications turn these bad boys into makeshift dab rigs with digital temperature control buttons. Pairing both types of hookahs together in one's garage lets stoners continue getting high while other guests smoke tobacco. They're great for parties!

## G-bongs

**Party Crashers:**

Parties devoid of patrons with the budget or access to professional glassware drove people to build gravity bongs. These disposable pipes were improvised onsite. The first two designs below evolved into the modern volcano pack and gravity hookah, so they're not entirely obsolete after all! Bucket bongs remain unchallenged to this day.

Parachute Bongs: Lungs

Slice bottom off a plastic bottle. Unscrew lid to fashion bowls. Water bottles get foil perforated by thumb tacks. Sports drinks demand more engineering skills. Cut a hole smaller than your socket/aerator combo and shove it in. Tape bread bag underneath bong and deflate lung back into bottle. Light bowl until there's a satisfactory smoke cloud. Unscrew cap and toke, toke, toke! Note: Lungs are dry bongs devoid of water.

Waterfall Bongs: Pissers

Similar bowls on next two designs. Punch a hole at the bottom, cork it shut and fill with water. Duct tape won't work because once you can only reapply it once all the water drains out. Pull the plug while lighting bowl until a sizeable hit is readied. Shove stopper back in and unscrew cap to inhale. Restore waterline before refilling bowl.

Bucket Bong: Cups

Slice bottom off bottle. Immerse container partially underwater in bucket. Pull up while lighting, but don't completely surface off waterline. Unscrew cap and toke.

# Dabbing Rigs

## Temperance

**Seasons' Greetings:**

Fire a butane torch underneath the nails until they glow red hot. Apply oil via dabber 3-5 times. Avoid using olive oil or wasting top-shelf wax! Instead, rely on distillate, preferably CBD. Coconut oil is an inferior substitute. Desperate potheads can dunk their pieces in ice water, reheat them and repeat the previous steps several times.

**Stoner Ninjitsu:**

Temperatures are listed in the next subsection. Load cold-starts before heating nails. The rest go in afterwards. Waive temperature guns at nails to determine if they're ready. Apply carb caps during hits to prevent dabs from cooling and remove them before you finish. Don't hold them in after you inhale them. If there's too much vapor to clear, pass the rig to another participant in the smoke circle before it turns stale.

**Trial by Fire:**

Fallout leftover from heavy use can be eradicated by simply heating nails until residue evaporates. Eventually, white-colored oxidation builds up over time through heavy usage. Simply dip the superheated nail in tap water while it's still hot to remove it.

## Temperature

**Riding the Hydra:**

Low-temp: 350-450°F

Bangers. Top-shelf, $CO_2$ extractions deserve cold-starts. Essential for live sugar (sugar diamonds), sugar wax, nectar and sap. Maximum flavor at the expense of smaller vapor clouds. Yet, the terpenes produce an entourage effect bolstering one's highs.

Mid-temp: 450-550°F

Standard. Gives balance to the mid-grade, ethanol extraction process. A necessity towards consuming rosin diamonds, crumble wax, live resin and rosin. Most of the terpene content remains intact and more vapor is produced at higher temperatures.

High-temp: 550-650°F

Hot dabs. Entry-level dabs are extracted through petroleum-based solvents such as isopropyl, butane, propane and acetone. Best suited for shatter, taffy and hard wax. Avoid temperatures exceeding 600°F as it increases the risk of burning your lungs.

# Review

## Armageddon

**Smoke Signals:**

Lighting bowls with hemp wicks mutes the taste of lighter fluid. Stand and gently inhale from bongs during tabletop sessions. Couch potatoes tilt bongs backwards diagonally, but never do so on rigs. Nails harbor dabs, that once liquified, easily spill.

**Texas Hold 'Em:**

Next rule, no coughing allowed in bongs! Force offenders to clean them. Whoever can't clear a cloud in one rip must purge it by either blowing it out as waste or finish the stale hit before passing. Arrogance is punished by ghosting. Guilty members must inhale dark-colored clouds and hold them in until they exhale nothing but clean air.

**Gentleman's Club:**

Let's repurpose tobacco pipes for CBD flower! Corncob pipes became iconic because of Douglas MacArthur and Popeye the Sailor Man. Shirlock Holmes paced around holding his Cabalash. J.R.R. Tolkien pondered new ideas while puffing on a billiard. You can fasten together a metal socket pipe, but its bowl requires a faucet aerator.

## Aftermath

**Peer Pressure:**

Visitors need to clean up after themselves. This includes picking up dishes, throwing away food scraps and washing ash dropped on the ground. Don't heckle individuals with health problems or responsibilities into getting higher than what's acceptable.

**Chemical Warfare:**

Scrape bowls free of resin and perform a quick rinse with tap water. Pour a modest amount of isopropyl (91%+) in pipes, toss some sea salt in and plug the ends shut. Remove anything metal, microwave for 30 seconds at a time, shake vigorously and rinse once satisfied. Metallic slides must be cleaned by hand in the same manner.

# CHAPTER TWELVE
## *Rolling Thunder*

### Quadrant 4:2

Listed below is this chapter's section directory. Topics are grouped together in subsections labeled by underlined bullets. Any further subdivision of information is organized into verses marked by bolded bullets.

Overview .................................................................................... 90

Joint Ventures ............................................................................ 91

Blunt Operations ....................................................................... 92

Dutch Underground .................................................................. 93

Safety Meetings ......................................................................... 94

Review ....................................................................................... 96

# Overview

## Frontiers

**Keef Command:**

You can consume concentrates on their own, but flower needs its keef. Regardless, bowls filled with torn nuggets or rolls stuffed full of ground weed need those glorious crystals. It cools smoke, controls the burn and leads to a smoother experience. Minor cannabinoids prevent racing heart rates, shortness of breath and potential anxiety. Also, there's a way to roll straight kif or moonrocks to supercharge smoke sessions!

## Pioneers

**High and Dry:**

A water bong's bowl can tolerate uncured weed, but rolls offer no forgiveness to the inexperienced. In the absence of dry-cured bud, heat an oven on warming (WM) to flash-cure nuggets. Give blunts 5-10 min, sweets 10-15 min and joints at 15-20 min.

**Hustle n' Grind:**

Every grinder is different. Some models let users swap plates limiting fineness. Cured bud is prone to pulverizing faster than flash-frozen nuggets. Practice perfecting your skills and always start with one quarter turn. Pre-milled flower should always be sold coarse-ground because customers can refine it further, but cannot undo finer grades.

<u>Coarse</u>: Blunts. Cannagars, dutches and backwoods.

<u>Medium</u>: Sweets. Swisher cigarillos and packs of minis.

<u>Fine</u>: Reefers. Joints or spliffs. Hemp papers are preferred.

**Chopped n' Screwed:**

Work stations require a rolling tray, grinder and laminated card. Always invest in quality brands of wraps, papers or cigars of choice. Follow the steps in this chapter to the tee before attempting anything on your own. Rolling several days' worth of joints or blunts makes life easier. Stash stockpiles in baggies so they don't dry out.

# Joint Ventures

## Boot Camp

**Off-the-walls:**

Josh Kesselman, founder of RAW papers, convinced smoke shops to stock pre-rolls for beginners. He made sure future generations, ones jaded by dabbing and vaping, had access to every accessory so the art of rolling wouldn't fall into utter obscurity.

**Tip-top Shape:**

Let's begin by rolling a cone with a filter! Properly rolled joints don't require these crutches, so I'm only going to show you the easiest method: Coils. Girth is dependent on the reefer's size. It requires rolling and unraveling both ends until you reach the crutch resembles a Torah scroll on a podium. Then, continue rocking them until you fabricate what resembles the coils found on a vintage, muscle car's cigarette lighter.

**Rite of Passage:**

Practice making pinners (0.25 g), doobies (0.5 g) and fatties (1 g). RAW supplies a cone maker. Position larger papers higher up. Insert crutches at the bottom with part of them remaining visible as they dangle below. Roll papers around these diagonally so gum lines (adhesive) don't line up. Use the built-in packer tool to compress weed. Add and pack more if necessary, but do leave enough space to twist the end shut.

## Black Ops

**Lost in Translation:**

Most rolling machines can handle 1.5 g comfortably. Measure the length of papers compared to the device. This determines how far up to place the crutch. Next, pour weed in until it reaches the other end and lightly packing everything down. Then, close your machine and roll it one direction for a few seconds. Feed papers with their adhesive facing you. Lick it right before feeding it in and perform several rotations.

**Holy Rollers:**

Personally, I join two papers together and shove 2 g in without a filter. Form a cradle at the bottom third (widthwise) keeping weed in the central half (lengthwise). Rock it back and forth, but leave some length on the short end of your paper so you tuck the bottom lip. Lay it on a flat surface and give edges the most pressure while rolling. Lick your finger to active adhesive, press facing down. And twist ends shut. Blot your tongue over stubborn spots. Add pieces of torn, wet paper to repair any damage.

# Blunt Operations

## Tabaqueros

### American Aficionados:

Indian workers smuggled pot to the Caribbean by masking its scent with tobacco, just like how Columbian coffee provided cover for Latin American cocaine operations. Rolling papers weren't as readily available to most locals, but cigars were plentiful. Over time, Jamaica's love for blunts was shared by the U.S. black population as well.

### Living by the Sword:

Before modern hybrids were crossbred into existence, most local landraces produced strong head highs. Nicotine helps quell anxiety and many rural, blue-collar workers smoked tobacco anyway. Unfortunately, this young man's drug cannot be sustained forever in someone's life without encountering potential health problems. Addicts weaning off or those who quit smoking do best leaning towards hemp-based paper.

## Torcedores

### Bold Boncheros:

Blunt rolling machines can easily stuff an eighth in a full-sized blunt, but we're going to start small by giving a sweet a teenth. Practitioners can substitute tobacco paper for hemp-derived wraps. Apart from being unfiltered, modify the steps from joint rollers. Similar to cones, people have the option of rolling their papers crooked. Don't blot over sections that don't adhere. Instead, keep licking them underneath the flaps.

### Peanut Gallery:

Time to roll a blunt! Grab a pack of backwoods or phillies. Remoisten stale packs by rubbing water over them. Stocking razor blades is optimal, but anyone regardless of how long their thumbs' fingernails are can split blunts open. Soak their seams before cracking and dump filler. Pack weed down by rocking it, slowly tuck the bottom lip starting at its mouthpiece. Continue repeating these steps upwards until finished. Follow the same procedure from earlier when tackling stubborn sections. Let it dry.

### Jailhouse Rock:

Inmates pioneered methods to secretly manufacture DYI cigar wraps in prison cells. Pour coffee or hot cocoa mix in a container. Mix enough water to create a viscosity you deem capable of soaking brown, paper napkins without being too watery. After marinating wraps, allow time to air dry. Lay two layers together to reinforce them.

# Dutch Underground

## Cannagars

**Pulp Fiction:**

King Palm manufactures leaf wraps without tobacco, but these wraps are not from true palms. In fact, cordia and tendu are used instead. Ironically, they're considered false palms by many. People don't even have to roll them, they just pack their tubes! Palm wraps are easier to prep than any other cigars, but pulp paper wins on pricing.

**Cubans Going Dutch:**

Cuban-American immigrants engineered this wonderful work of art! They consider it more of a cannagar than a blunt. Tobacco-leaf cigars must always be rolled diagonally like cones. Ensure the outer parts of the leaves face their rollers. A sun-grown binder leaf, cloud-grown wrapper leaf and tree sap is recommended. Slice binder leaf flush after rolling and do the same for the wrapper. Sap supplants saliva as an adhesive.

## Thai Sticks

**Traditional Burial:**

A practice dating back to antiquity has been revived! Fresh, landrace sativa isn't given time to dry before being run through by bamboo skewers. Fan leaves are wrapped over these sticks by tightly coiling a hemp wick around the packed bud. Carefully remove stems puncturing wraps so nuggets don't fall apart. Bury everything for three months to initiate a cure. Remove twine to unravel protective wrapping. Wax is a safer alternative to opium. Rub it over the cigar, let it dry and slowly pull skewers out.

**Contemporary Method:**

Molds shave time off the shaping process. Hemp stalks and parchment paper are more accessible options in developed countries. Shove vacuum sealed sticks in the fridge for two weeks. Take the parchment paper off them whenever you smoke one!

**Royal Highness:**

Drug labs repurpose flash-frozen sugar leaves as cannagar wraps. Our homegrown beginners should start with fan leaves instead because they're easier. Devein blades, lay them in squares and apply rosin to join them together. Wrap individual patches over Thai sticks, not entire sheets, applying rosin whenever necessary. I recommend allowing cigars to age two months. Humidity packs can help maintain the 135 rule. Ideally, adding the temperature and relative humidity (RH) together gives us 135.

# Safety Meetings

## Joints

**Double Vision:**

For unfiltered joints, select one end to serve as the mouthpiece. Usually, they'll have a longer, more tapered side. Sometimes, the shorter end may be more compacted making it better at preventing debris from falling out during puffs. Occasionally, both sites look almost identical. In that circumstance, unravel both ends before deciding.

**Heads or Tails:**

Slice the end off of a cotton swab and use it to slowly pack the weed in your joint's mouthpiece. Wooden versions are easier to cut than the plastic kind. Gently massage piece until you've created what resembles a musical reed. There are two options for prepping the other end. Option A: Leave it alone. This works if you haven't already unraveled both sides. Option B: Unravel and pack end with the swab. Some people repurpose their roach paper to patch holes in blunts, but fresh paper tastes better.

**Circle of Life:**

Leave roaches/butts outside overnight to air out. Otherwise, they'll stink up rooms. Whoever cannot do so should seal them in an air-tight baggie inside a container. Set them in a position where they won't get wet, roll away in the wind or get stolen. Losing dro is costly and nobody wants to see children get sick from consuming them. Remember: The longer someone waits to smoke them, the more bitter they become.

## Cannagars

**Have a Cigar:**

A double guillotine is the optimum cigar cutter. Cigars are held together by a line forming a ring along their mouthpieces. Be sure to never cut past that area. Place the bottom side firmly on the blade. Bring the other blade down gently until it makes contact. Rotate cigar so the blade begins digging in. Once seated, slice that end off!

**Cutting the Mustard:**

<u>Straight</u>: Guillotines give small, boxed-pressed options a generous draw.

<u>Wedge</u>: Spring-loaded cutters are used on mid-sized, tapered cigar designs.

<u>Punch</u>: Bullets prevent debris from falling out of large, round cannagars.

<u>Scissor</u>: Not recommended. A razor blade is a far superior option.

## Indulgence

### Passing the Torch:

Joints with uncut ends need continuous flame application. Users shouldn't inhale the first drag and wait until taste improves before counting actual hits. Take time lighting cannagars with soft-flame lighters at a distance until they're ready. Rollers are given the first hit, aka greens. Guests of honor, such as superiors, elders and patrons call backdoor. Everyone else falls in line according to seniority or first come, first serve.

### No Flying Dutchman:

Wipe your lips beforehand; absolutely no lippin' allowed! Coincidentally, sticking the object too deep in one's mouth, especially while suffering from cottonmouth (dry-mouth induced by getting high), causes the piece to stick to their bottom lip. One sudden jerk, it rips wide open spilling everywhere and potentially making burn holes.

### Puffing the Magic Dragon:

Take long, slow drags to reduce uneven burning. Smoke is held in one's mouth prior to inhaling. This lets it cool and helps adjust for expansion. Some strains perform differently. Unlike dabs or vapes, hold hits in for up to 3-5 seconds (Indian hits). Exhaling through your nose shouldn't be performed with blunts because tobacco encourages stuffy noses. Take two hits and then pass it to the left (puff, puff, pass).

## Etiquette

### Texas Hold 'Em:

Don't rush gatherings by passing numerous blunts; just give each their own personal stick! Anyone hogging or slowing down rotation is chiefin', something which is only tolerated if permission is granted ahead of time. Never pass anything that's been lipped! Whatever cannot be dried by a lighter must be sliced away by the offender.

### Steerage Class:

Running is corrected by simply lighting lagging areas until they even out. Let them burn before blowing them out. Repeated offenses occurring on one side of a blunt can warrant wetting them by dabbing saliva. Give it some time to dry before showing aggression. Use your lighter to accelerate the process. If a toothpick can't unplug a clogged mouthpiece, it's time to cut the dang end off. Don't tear, god forbid, bite it!

### Poop Deck:

Shotgunning can be performed two ways. First, by exhaling hits into a girl's mouth through a tunnel created by placing each other's hands together is sexy. Blowing it directly is basically kissing. Forcing smoke the opposite direction rolls are supposed to work generates bigger clouds without looking gay. In the absence of a pipe, roach clips let old heads kill roaches. All must reach an agreement before tossing them.

# Review

## Inebriation

**Buzzed:** Subclinical

Microdosing. A fix isn't a true high, so performance during work situations and class attendance won't be affected. Helps authors and musicians overcome writer's block.

**Stoned:** Euphoria

Enhances exercise and menial chores. Those behind the wheel still retain enough assertiveness to tackle aggressive traffic in major cities without feeling too stressed out. I do not advocate driving while intoxicated, but weed makes you more cautious.

**Blitzed:** Excitement

Afroman! Driving ability, motor skills and capacity to engage intelligent conversation remain uninhibited. Eyes become glazed and redden, which can draw unwanted attention from the public. Postpone errands for 30 minutes until sobriety increases.

**Baked:** Stupor

Driving skills and ability to fight vastly impaired. Not zooted enough to warrant trip sitters, but a wingman should serve as a designated driver. Renders participants only capable of watching movies or listening to music. They're incapable of acting sober.

**Faded:** Coma

Sativa users grow uncomfortably high, aka geeked, and risk greening out (getting sick). Indica often renders one couch-locked. Speech is soft, slurred and unintelligible. They might pass out and wake up still high. Crossfading is achieved by consuming alcohol.

## Enlightenment

Anyone counteracting greening, trying to sober up or continuing sessions without getting higher can roll spliffs of CBD-rich flower during daytime. Those preparing for sleep orient towards CBN. Both cannabinoids counteract THC's negative side effects.

# Summary

## *The White Market*

### Medicine

Replacing synthetics with plant-based medication not only works for controlled substances, but for most meds in general. Herbs, spices, roots, leaves, flowers, bark and mushrooms won't replace everything. Blood pressure medicine and hormone pills are prime examples. Natural medicine is more affordable with less side effects. Heck, it might drive the cost of healthcare down! The opioid crisis comes to an end, rural economies outside local incorporations are boosted and drug war finally over.

### Vanguards

Before Native Americans can implement *Saving the United States'* policies, they must complete Operation White Wolf. It's my plan to kick the idiotic non-natives who are destroying the U.S. out in 2-3 generations! To tackle that, they need to read *Native American Strategies*. Only then can we establish farms in rural communities on the outskirts of civilization. Since natives are required to pool capital prior to this, growing cannabis is the answer. They don't require subsidies or large plots of land!

### Closing

This concludes your presentation. For those wanting more, *The Early Church* is my next title. It's a technical handbook containing the directions on how to establish a Sabbatarian Church denomination for Protestant Gentiles and Messianic Jews. This global network gives members financial security and others free schools. As principal investigator and sole researcher of this research project, I'm signing off now. If you still need more resources, feel free to read my online bibliographies at any time.

# Conclusion

## Afterword

*Thank you for reading his book! When Robert started this project, he lacked a government grant or research team to aid him in his efforts. This man wasn't gainfully-employed for over a decade due to mental health problems. Food stamps was all he had and no other financial aid was available while conducting research. The author was forced to live off less than $100 a week.*

*Your support not only furthers this author's research, but also helps the indigenous people throughout the New World finally have a chance to break free from these Germanic/Anglo-Saxon civilizations destroying their countries.*

**-N.D.**

## Postface

*Cannabis Market was my response to the rise in legalized marijuana and hemp dispensaries. Without this book, it would be impossible for everyone to have access to quality products. Well-cured sativa and balanced hybrids reduce heart palpitations, breathing problems and strain on current indica supplies.*

*Across the globe, rampant medical avarice and outright dishonesty causes monopolization, enslavement, poisoning, bankruptcy and reduced economic productivity in the workforce. Therefore, I needed to address the dilemma.*

**-R.R.**

# Acknowledgements

*I would like to thank GOTCHA! LLP for editorial services and Kindle Direct Publishing for publishing my books. Special thanks to Streetlight Graphics who designed the signature "money tree" illustrations on my monogram pages.*

*Special mention to Unsplash.com for allowing their digital photography to used in my works. Each photographer will be given recognition on my website. My bibliographies list the websites I've drawn information from as sources.*

*I personally thank everyone who read my first book! Most importantly, I give God credit for everything. If it weren't for his divine guidance, I would've never succeeded in creating these models if I tried relying solely on my own efforts. Blessed be those who partake in Operation White Wolf and support my work.*

## Cannabis Market

*"The handbook educating enthusiasts how to properly cultivate and consume their medical marijuana or recreational cannabis products safely!"*

# CONTRIBUTIONS
## *Subsection Index*

About the Author ............................................................ 101

Glossary .......................................................................... 102

Colophon ........................................................................ 104

Endpiece ......................................................................... 105

Monogram ...................................................................... 106

# About the Author

*My name is Robert Robinson. I began life as a cowboy working on my family's ranch. As I reached middle school, I joined the Civil Air Patrol. The U.S. Air Force's auxiliary interested me so much that I began studying military history. During high school, I opened a landscaping business and named it Robinson's Landscaping. It was never legally-registered nor did it ever hire more than two employees, most of the time only serving as temporary help.*

*I was awarded two degrees in applied science at The Art Institute of Houston after graduating from the Class of '05 at Montgomery High School (MISD) in Montgomery, Texas. The first certificate was my Associate of Restaurant Catering and Management. Upon returning, I earned a bachelor's degree in Hospitality Management. During my time in the industry, I worked as a line cook, prep cook, expeditor (expo), waiter, host, busser and delivery driver.*

*Afterwards, I focused on my research to save Western civilization. I've played drums since the year 2000 and am an avid music enthusiast. I also diet and weight train as a form of physical rehabilitation, something I've had to do twice from being drugged and bewitched by others. I'm using my experience and research in lieu of education to touch on these post-doctoral topics.*

# Glossary

### Aeroponics

Irrigation systems designed to grow plants without the use of mediums. They're suspended midair while their roots are sprayed with nutrient solution. Commercial systems combine high-pressure pumps and digital POS systems called biological systems matrixes. Partial aeroponics combines growing mediums for cannabis plants.

### Aquaculture

Aquatic farms rearing marine life. Freshwater hatcheries usually run along dams. Brackish and saltwater farms are most often found in river deltas or coastal wetlands. Fish released into the wild once caught aren't farm-raised; they're 100% wild-caught!

### Aquaponics

Irrigation systems combining aquaculture and hydroponics. A deep water culture hydroponics system works in conjunction with a marine fish tank. Animal waste supplies nutrients and the plumbing system purifies nutrient solution before feeding.

### Bubbleponics

Hydroponics system combining two others together: A reciprocating deep water culture and drip line. RDWCs contain an airstone oxygenating nutrient solutions in reservoirs and sprayers feeding unsubmerged roots. Drip systems soak roots inside grow mediums. Bubbletotes are multi-plant kits and bubblebuckets house one plant.

### Deep Water Culture

DWC systems feature a nutrient tank with less than a foot of solution. Styrofoam platforms for pots float on the surface. These containers house plants in mediums. Also known as deep flow technique (DFT), floating raft technology (FRT) or raceway.

### Drip Line System

Hydroponics system running a drip line above containers. Inner meadows transplant saplings or plants grown solely in mineral wool rely upon them! Nutrient solution is top-fed over their growing medium. Hydroton and rockwool are preferred as they retain moisture better. Drip lines combined with RDWCs created bubbleponics kits.

### Dutch Bucket System

A DWC hydroponics system resulting in a chain of buckets connected by PVC tubing. My Dutch bubblebucket system upgrades DWC systems to the bubbleponics version. Buckets give the plants' roots more room and prevent them from becoming tangled.

## Ebb and Flow

Passive hydroponics system alternating between periodic flooding and draining intervals. Water pumps circulate nutrient solution from reservoir tanks to planter boxes. Their plants are suspended in containers filled with porous growing medium.

## Hydroponics

Plumbing systems designed to grow plants without the use of soil. They're raised in growing mediums (Hydroton, perlite, rockwool) and fed a nutrient solution (nutrients mixed into water, aka "nutes"). Taproots are given a supply of air to prevent root rot.

## Kratky Method

Passive hydroponics system combining a garden pot with a growing medium above a container, which serves as a partially-filled nutrient reservoir with air up top. Roots drop through holes to the solution below. As water levels drop, air supply increases.

## Natural Rating

Used on the park system's timber plots. Timber is sprayed with natural plant-based treatment and sealant once harvested. Choosing natural ratings on timber is better for the environment they grow in. This reduces chemicals found in their rain runoff.

## Nutrient Film Technique

NFT hydroponics systems are shallow PVC raceways that pump a current of nutrient solution. It's so shallow and resembles thin film. Tubing curves to create staggered rows. Gravity also helps assist streams. Strainer baskets require a growing medium.

## Non-GMO Rating

Genetically-modified organisms, aka GMOs, allowed corn to go from maize to yellow sweet corn. Resilience to pests and yields abounded, but flavor diminished over time. Triploid cannabis is a prime example. People need to stop playing god with nature!

## Shallow Water Culture

Passive hydroponics system similar to DWCs with nutrient tanks filled 8-10 inches full. Seeds are dipped in rooting hormone and inserted into the floating rockwool cubes.

## Organic Rating

Medicinal herbs can be used in place of antibiotics. Plant-based insect repellents supplant pesticides. Duck runs help eliminate some pests before organic plant-based pesticides are sprayed. Compost, aged manure and worm castings are their fertilizer.

## Wick Method

Passive hydroponics method similar to Kratky, but with a wick running between two containers stacked on top of one another. Outer meadow's transplant containers.

# Colophon

**Graphic Design Group**

Graphic Design, Covers

TAX TREES: THE LANDSCAPER'S BIBLE, (ed. 3)

TAX TREES: SAVING THE UNITED STATES, (ed. 1)

TAX TREES: NATIVE AMERCIAN STRATEGIES, (ed. 1)

**Kindle Direct Publishing**

Publishing, Marketing

TAX TREES: technical handbook trilogy (ed. 1-2)

BJÖRK'S ADVENTURE, parody thriller novel (ed. 1)

MY DIRE STRAITS, author's memoir (ed. 1-2)

CANNABIS MARKET, technical handbook (ed. 1)

THE EARLY CHURCH, technical handbook (ed. 1)

BEER MATH, technical handbook (ed. 1)

**Amazon.com, Inc.**

Printing, Distribution

TAX TREES: THE LANDSCAPER'S BIBLE, (ed. 1-3)

TAX TREES, technical handbook trilogy (ed. 1)

BJÖRK'S ADVENTURE, parody thriller novel (ed. 1)

MY DIRE STRAITS, author's memoir (ed. 1)

CANNABIS MARKET, technical handbook (ed. 1)

THE EARLY CHURCH, technical handbook (ed. 1)

2012 Copyright: TXU 1-821-070

https://robertrobinsonjr.com

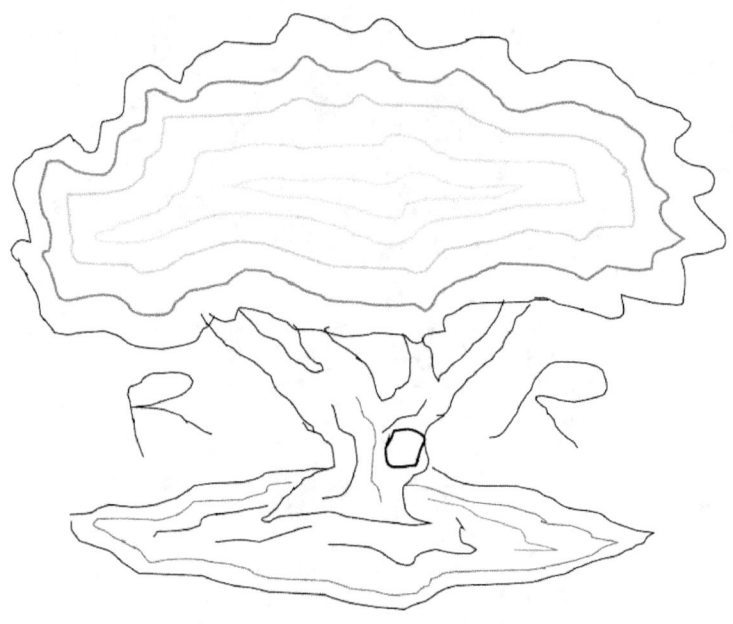

www.ingramcontent.com/pod-product-compliance
Lightning Source LLC
Chambersburg PA
CBHW070804220526
45466CB00002B/540